POWER
OF A
RICH READING
CLASSROOM

THE
POWER
OF A
RICH READING
CLASSROOM

BY THE CENTRE FOR LITERACY IN PRIMARY EDUCATION

CORWIN

A SAGE company
2455 Teller Road
Thousand Oaks, California 91320
(0800)233-9936
www.corwin.com

SAGE Publications Ltd
1 Oliver's Yard
55 City Road
London EC1Y 1SP

SAGE Publications India Pvt Ltd
B 1/I 1 Mohan Cooperative Industrial Area
Mathura Road
New Delhi 110 044

SAGE Publications Asia-Pacific Pte Ltd
3 Church Street
#10-04 Samsung Hub
Singapore 049483

Editor: Amy Thornton
Senior project editor: Chris Marke
Project management: Deer Park Productions
Marketing manager: Dilhara Attygalle
Cover design: Wendy Scott
Typeset by: C&M Digitals (P) Ltd, Chennai, India
Printed in the UK by Ashford Colour Press Ltd.

Library of Congress Control Number: 2019954065

British Library Cataloguing in Publication data

A catalogue record for this book is available from the
British Library

ISBN 978-1-5264-9178-7
ISBN 978-1-5264-9177-0 (pbk)

At SAGE we take sustainability seriously. Most of our products are printed in the UK using responsibly sourced
papers and boards. When we print overseas we ensure sustainable papers are used as measured by the PREPS
grading system. We undertake an annual audit to monitor our sustainability.

CONTENTS

ABOUT THE CLPE

CLPE

CENTRE FOR **LITERACY**
IN PRIMARY EDUCATION

This book is produced by the Centre for Literacy in Primary Education (CLPE) a UK charity dedicated to improving the teaching of literacy in primary schools.

The charity has been in existence since 1972 and has a national and international reputation for the quality of its work and research. CLPE is based in London, England in a building which houses a library of 23,000 carefully chosen children's books and provides training and teaching resources for primary schools to help them to teach literacy creatively and effectively. The charity works face to face with around 2,000 teachers each year delivering training courses at the centre in London and around the country supporting teachers to understand all aspects of literacy development and to put quality children's literature at the heart of learning. CLPE writes and provides a range of online resources to support the teaching of literacy; these are all designed to support teachers' knowledge about children's literature, its creators and how to use it in the classroom.

In the face to face and online work CLPE makes research and evidence on pedagogy, subject knowledge and effective strategies accessible and visible. The charity aims to make the links between teachers learning and pupil learning explicit, showing how new knowledge and skills will impact on pupil progress and attainment.

CLPE's work has always added to the knowledge base around children's literacy and the effective teaching of literacy, undertaking research about literacy, literature and the best classroom practice to support children to become confident, happy and enthusiastic readers and writers, with all the benefits this brings.

To find out more visit https://clpe.org.uk/

ABOUT THE AUTHORS

Each chapter in this book is written by one of the experienced staff at CLPE. The foreword is written by Aidan Chambers, a patron of CLPE whose work has inspired countless teachers and children. The editor of this book is Louise Johns-Shepherd, CLPE's Chief Executive.

Aidan Chambers

Aidan Chambers is an award winning author of children's books and texts for teachers and librarians. His work has inspired generations of children and teachers and continues to inspire the work of the CLPE. Aidan is a Patron of CLPE.

Louise Johns-Shepherd – Chief Executive

Louise joined CLPE as the Chief Executive in 2013. She has worked in education for thirty years and was the headteacher of two schools, a nursery school and a primary school. She also worked in education policy and was a senior leader in both the Primary National Strategies and the National College of School Leadership.

Charlotte Hacking – Learning Programme Leader

Charlotte joined CLPE in 2012 having taught across the primary school age range and been a leader in several primary schools. She leads the CLPE's ground breaking Power of Pictures research and developed the CLPE's Power of Poetry research project. She is an expert in the use of picture books across primary schools and the teaching of poetry.

Ann Lazim – Library and Literature Manager

Ann has been the librarian at CLPE for nearly 30 years. She is a qualified children's librarian and has an MA in Children's Literature. Ann curates the library at CLPE and the Core Books online resource. She has a wealth of knowledge about children's literature and a particular interest in international children's literature and traditional tales.

Darren Matthews – Primary Advisory Teacher

Darren is an experienced teacher who has taught across all phases in a range of London primary schools and held a wide number of different leadership posts. Darren worked for many years as an Associate Teacher for Power of Reading before joining the permanent team in 2016. Darren is a drama specialist and leads CLPE's Raising Achievement in Writing programme.

Katie Myles – Primary Advisory Teacher

Katie joined CLPE in 2015 and is a member of the expert teaching team and an experienced teacher who has taught across the primary phases. She leads CLPE's English Subject Leader programmes as well as developing cross-curricular programmes with fiction at their heart.

Anjali Patel – Lead Advisory Teacher

Before joining CLPE in 2014 Anjali worked in teaching and leadership positions throughout the primary age range. Her expertise is in Early Years and early reading development and she writes regularly for a range of publications such as *Teach Early Years* and *BBC Bitesize* as well as leading on the development of CLPE's Early Years programmes.

Dr Jonny Rodgers – Primary Advisory Teacher

Jonny was the Head of a Power of Reading school before joining the CLPE team in 2016. He is an experienced teacher and senior leader, who has taught across the primary age range. Jonny has a doctorate in linguistics and leads the CLPE NQT programme.

Farrah Serroukh – Learning Programme Leader

Farrah joined CLPE in 2013. Before that she taught across the primary school age range and held several leadership posts. She is the author of CLPE's Reflecting Realities Survey and leads the ground breaking and award winning work in this area. She is an expert on the teaching of children whose first language is not English.

FOREWORD

Everything changes, except what fundamentally matters, which always remains the same.

I've been a teacher in various sectors of education since 1955. In that time I've heard the same questions asked about reading and children. How should it be taught? The vast majority of children read very little; how can we help them become keen readers? Does it matter what they read? Why bother anyway?

What people who say 'they don't read' meant in the 1950s, and still do mean, is that 'they' don't read what we think they should read. This has never changed, ever, not from the first days of written and printed words till today. In fact, the young read and write more now than they ever have done. Think of 'social media': text messages, Facebook, Twitter, WhatsApp, etc., etc., etc. Endless writing and reading, not only of words but of visual images.

Another change: in the 1950s you could leave school only functionally literate and still get a reasonably good job. Coal miners like my maternal grandfather could hardly read and write and didn't need to. My father left school aged fourteen with no paper qualification, trained as a joiner and ended his career managing a funeral department at the Co-operative Society. And here is a marker of the change since the 1950s. My father's successor as a department manager was required to have a qualification in business and funeral management.

The fact is that these days, unless you can write and read with great facility and cope with the complex writing and reading required by our computerised culture, you will be a third-class citizen. You are more likely to be out of work than those who are sophisticatedly literate. If you have a job, it is likely to be the kind that competent readers and writers don't want to do. Proficiency in reading and writing is not now an optional extra. It is fundamentally necessary. It is life-determining.

But what do we mean by 'read' and 'reading'? Is it enough to bore your way through texts, it doesn't matter what kind? Or does it make a difference what you read? And if so, why? (Same questions again!)

All reading involves interpretation: working out what the text means. What it *seems* to mean (superficially) and what it *actually* means. Ambiguity is at play in every text of every kind. Knowing how to interpret is an essential feature of reading. Let's call it, reading with thoughtful, discriminating and critical understanding.

We learn about this with the help of those who already know how to do it, which in our culture means with a teacher. Reading is a cultural activity; it is not genetically controlled: we are not born to be readers and writers. The human race invented both. And like all cultural activity, we learn by imitation. We learn to speak by imitating the sounds made by those who look after us when we are born and as we grow up. Similarly, we learn how to be a reader by imitating those who are already readers. Which means we tend to become readers like those we imitate. Ergo, it matters how good as readers those who teach us are themselves.

Reading is often said to be a private, solitary activity. People who say this are thinking of the time spent passing our eyes over words and images, doing it in silence (reading quietly for ourselves). But that is only a small part of our lives as readers. In fact, reading is a social activity. We choose what we read after hearing about a text from friends, from radio or tv or from social media. And we cannot help talking about what we read when it matters to us more than as a pastime activity. We feel impelled to share with friends, relatives, teachers, anybody. You could say that reading begins and ends with talk.

For teachers, this means a number of features have to be present in the effort to help pupils become thoughtful, discriminating readers who enjoy reading.

The first feature is that texts must be easily available. Books, to mention the old and still best form for deep rather than superficial reading, have to be there – around us – in large numbers and variety. And we have to be able to get at them easily. They have to be accessible, not shut away and hard to get at.

Next, we become readers by imitating, 'by hearing it done'. One change that has happened in recent times proves this beyond mere opinion: the neuroscientists who specialise in what happens in our brains while we are reading have shown how being read to helps open up the 'pathways' that make it possible for us to become readers. Reading aloud is essential.

Third, everyone needs time to read for themselves, otherwise we never become committed readers. For many pupils, perhaps the majority, the only place where this can be done without interruption and regularly is in school. Time for pupils to read for themselves in school is essential.

Fourth, because talk matters, teachers need to be skilled in the kind of talk about what has been read that best helps their pupils grow.

One final point. The texts which contain everything we need to become sophisticated readers are those we usually call 'literature'. By which I mean stories of all kinds, poetry, those visual texts we call picturebooks. Words and pictures composed as narratives. Why is this so? Because these texts are the ones that offer the most complex and profound of meanings. They are the ones which, by attending closely to them, we discover how to interpret meaning in the richest, most aware manner. That's why it matters what our pupils read. "I am what I read. And I read to find out who I am."

There is nothing more important in education than helping learners of all ages to develop as readers and writers. That is what this book is about, and I commend it to you.

Aidan Chambers

INTRODUCTION

This is a book about creating an environment for reading in your classroom that supports children to become engaged and successful readers. Our hope is that it will help you to have a picture of the whole reading process and that you will have ideas about how to implement what you have learnt in your classroom. Our aim is to produce a practical handbook which highlights the recent and relevant research and which supports you to understand how different texts and pedagogical approaches are useful, supportive and transformational at particular ages and stages.

If you are reading this book you probably already know how important it is to ensure that children become literate but more than that, that they enjoy their literacy. Teaching children to become confident and competent readers and writers is surely the most important thing that primary school teachers do, it quite literally changes children's lives. And this is why we at the Centre for Literacy in Primary Education do what we do. Our charity exists only to support the teaching of literacy; everything we publish, every training session we run, every resource we make is created with the purpose of ensuring primary school teachers have what they need to help children in their classes to become and to recognise themselves as readers and writers.

What is the main thing we need to support our teaching of reading? Books of course. Books with stories, with poetry, with characters and with illustrations that will encourage engagement whoever you are and whatever your starting point. Texts that take you to new worlds and introduce you to new people – real and imagined, that help you to discover patterns and constructions in language and bring you new ideas and understanding. Alongside books you need a range of experiences to help you discover and respond to those books in a variety of ways – privately or as a shared endeavour – and skills that enable you to decode the text, make sense of the construction and allow you to respond to the experience. All of these things are what we need to provide in a rich reading classroom and we have tried to describe them and provide practical advice for implementing them in this book.

CLPE has been working in the field of children's literacy since 1972. This book builds on the research heritage, knowledge and understanding of nearly fifty years of practice. CLPE and those who have worked for the charity are responsible for some of the most ground-breaking work and publications in this area of learning. This book references seminal texts such as *The Reader in the Writer* (Barrs and Cork), *Understanding Spelling* (O'Sullivan), *A Year with Poetry* (Barrs and Rosen) and *The CLPE Reading Book* (Thomas). Our work today is still underpinned by the thinking and research that took place in order to produce those books.

Throughout its existence, CLPE has pioneered approaches to formative, observation-based assessment in literacy. Between 1985 and 1987 Myra Barrs and her colleagues worked with large numbers of teachers working in inner London primary schools and developed The Primary Language Record (PLR) and then The Primary Learning Record. These assessment records were almost immediately recommended by the Cox Committee, which developed the English National Curriculum, as a model for a national system of recordkeeping. The Primary Language Record went on to influence language and literacy records in all parts of the UK and become an accepted means of assessment for the English National Curriculum. The PLR was accompanied by four five-point scales, two in reading and two in writing which teachers found extremely helpful for assessment but also for planning and understanding progression. However, with the introduction of standard assessment tests and the associated levels and sub-levels these scales fell out of use as an assessment although they continued to be referenced by many teachers and academics.

In 2015 CLPE worked with all the major English Subject Associations to redevelop these scales into a supportive and useful tool to help teachers understand progression in reading and writing. The new Reading and Writing Scales describe the journeys that children make in order to become literate. They distil the complex and individual patterns of progress into accessible and informative scales. The purpose of the scales is to help teachers to understand what progression looks like in reading and writing and to illustrate how schools can plan to provide an environment that supports children's development as readers and writers. The pedagogy underpinning the scales is grounded in a coherent theory of children's language and literacy development, they are designed to support and develop teacher subject knowledge in literacy development, not to set out a linear sequence of targets that children need to reach in order to move to the next phase.

We reference these scales (which are freely available on our website) throughout this book and they underpin all aspects of our day-to-day work at CLPE. What we hope to do with the scales, and this book is to strengthen teacher understanding and subject knowledge in the development of reading and writing. We recognise that children all have very different learning patterns but hope that by providing a common framework we will help teachers to plan for the varying needs of individual children as they become literate.

When you're thinking about building a rich reading classroom you will need to think about the texts and the literature you want in your classroom, this is the foundation of your curriculum and the most important aspect of any reading classroom. You'll also need to think about how you want to present those texts, what messages your classroom and teaching are going to give the young readers who are learning in it, how you will create a rich reading experience and how you'll ensure that the children in your class are taught the skills they need to become competent and confident readers and writers.

We've structured this book into three parts. The first part deals with the choices you as a teacher have to make when you are choosing the literature that your class will come across whilst they are with you. The second part looks at some key and essential aspects that you need to consider when thinking about the teaching approaches you are going to take in your classroom. In the final part we unpick the use of high quality literature for each age group. This part offers practical ideas to support you to embed the text experience as well as ideas for teaching linked skills such as comprehension, phonics, spelling and grammar in a rich reading and broad curriculum. There are also ideas and examples of how to embed authentic writing within your curriculum and to link it to your reading teaching.

PART 1 – CHOOSING HIGH QUALITY LITERATURE IN THE PRIMARY SCHOOL CLASSROOM

At CLPE we believe that the use of high quality books as the bedrock of an English curriculum is at the heart of a school's successful approach to engage and support children to become motivated and independent readers. In order to recommend appropriate books to children, to extend and develop their reading and continue to feed their interests, adults working in schools need to have an extensive knowledge of the full range of children's literature available.

We know that there are books that lend themselves to being talked about, thought through, returned to and are engaging for children for many reasons. They tend to be texts with powerful stories that stir ideas and excite the reader's interest and imagination. They are books that children will want to re-read, and remember. It is books like these that you want at the centre of your curriculum.

We've started this part of our book with a chapter on ensuring that our book are truly reflecting the realities of your class and the world they live in. This is an underpinning principle for all our work and needs to be a principle for you as you build a classroom library or school book stock. Farrah Serroukh takes us through the reasons why in her chapter and also offers some useful advice about making decisions and developing reader identity.

The second chapter in this part is on Early Readers. Thinking about the particular needs of children who are just beginning their reading journeys is very important. Anjali Patel discusses some of the key things to think about with Early Readers and also suggests some key texts that are important for moving children to the next stage of development. When we are thinking about Early Readers we often assume they are the very youngest children in our care and this is usually the case. However, Anjali also considers those children who may be older but, for whatever reason, still at a stage where they are dependent on adult support.

It is important here to make sure we have in our repertoire some age-appropriate texts that will support these children as they progress.

At CLPE we are very lucky to have an experienced and trained children's librarian on our staff. Ann Lazim is the author of our chapters on choosing fiction and non-fiction. She sets out some important considerations when putting together both fiction and non-fiction collections and also helps us to understand what the key features of a good text look like.

The final two chapters in this part are on Picture Books and Poetry. In our work with schools we find that these two types of books are often overlooked, for very different reasons. Poetry is the poor relation of children's literature, often avoided or shoved into a short 'unit of work,' its transformational potential can be missed. Charlotte Hacking shares the key reasons that poetry should have a prominent place in every book corner as well as some examples of how to embed it within your daily routines.

It is tempting to think of Picturebooks as only having a place in Early Years or Key Stage One classrooms but in this chapter Charlotte takes us through the importance of the picture book as a unique and complex reading experience and shows how they are key to developing reading skills throughout the school into Key Stage Two and beyond.

PART 2 – ESSENTIAL TEACHING APPROACHES FOR A RICH READING CURRICULUM

This part unpicks key teaching approaches that you will help you to develop and extend children's understanding of the texts you have chosen to teach with.

The role and attitudes of teachers in creating a reading environment that reflects a commitment to developing readers with interests and agency and that promotes reading as a socially engaging activity that is valued is key to the engagement of children in the reading process. Book areas where books and information about books are displayed attractively and where browsing, choosing and reading can take place are a visible way of establishing and promoting a positive ethos for reading for pleasure. The reading environment is of course more than just a 'reading corner' and Katie Myles unpicks this in Chapter 7. A read aloud programme where children have shared experiences of texts and can hear that which they cannot yet read is a fundamental and integral part of any rich reading classroom as are adults who model and demonstrate what reading and writing looks like. Farrah Serroukh gives more details about building these approaches into your classroom planning in Chapters 8 and 10.

Helping children to respond to a text with creative approaches like role-play, drama, illustration, visualisation or graphic representation (like story mapping) will support them to experiment with ways that they can inhabit a fictional world. It enables children to put themselves into particular characters' shoes and imagine how things would look from that point of view. These kinds of approaches all give children the opportunity to imagine and understand plot, character and setting in ways that they can draw on later when they write. Darren Matthews looks at the importance of drama and how to plan for it within the English curriculum and Charlotte Hacking shows how reading illustration helps children to understand complex structures and concepts in picture books.

PART 3: USING HIGH QUALITY LITERATURE ACROSS THE PRIMARY SCHOOL – HOW IT WORKS

In this final part we try to show how to put all that has come before into practice. Our teaching team Anjali Patel, Katie Myles, Darren Matthews and Jonny Rodgers have each taken a phase of the primary school and for each of these phases they have set out what is distinctive about that age group in terms of their reading journey and what it is that teachers will need to consider in their planning.

Each chapter then suggests texts that support this age group and outlines how to use them in your classroom. For each phase we have tried to support you with texts and ideas for reading aloud, whole class study, reading into writing, group reading and individual or independent reading.

We have used these chapters to show how the books you choose and the ways in which you talk about them are key in developing age-range specific skills and to developing a community of reading and readers in your classroom.

Throughout this book we have, wherever we can, referenced our wider work or the excellent work of others in this field. We hope this book is useful for you and helps you to create a rich reading classroom but we know that you will need more detail about the research, more recommendations about appropriate texts or titles or further reading to help take your thinking forward. There are references at the end of each chapter which show the range of work we draw on a day-to-day basis and we urge you to do the same.

All of our work at CLPE is centred around the importance of quality children's literature. We know that to develop a rich reading classroom which in turn develops real readers you need to know books, you need to know stories, you need to want to delve and lose yourself in new and unfamiliar worlds, to view the discovery of new characters and new plots with wonder and excitement. If you can create children who feel like that then you have created a rich reading classroom. We hope that this book will help you to begin that journey.

Louise Johns-Shepherd

REFERENCES

Barrs, M. and Cork, V. (2001) *The Reader in the Writer*. London: CLPE

Barrs, M. and Rosen, M. (1997) *A Year with Poetry*. London: CLPE.

O'Sullivan, O. (2007) *Understanding Spelling*. London: Routledge.

Thomas, A. (1991) The Reading Book. London: CLPE.

PART 1

CHOOSING HIGH QUALITY LITERATURE IN THE PRIMARY SCHOOL CLASSROOM

CHAPTER 1

REFLECTING REALITIES: NURTURING READER IDENTITY

FARRAH SERROUKH

Take a moment to think of a memorable book from your childhood. What is it that made this book special? What was it about the book that spoke to you?

There is something quite magical about forming a connection to a book: the way in which the words on the page can conjure feelings of excitement, fun, joy, laughter or tears, channelling the part of our being that fundamentally makes us human.

As educators, we invest a great deal of time and energy in ensuring children learn to navigate the words on the page so that they can draw meaning from the text. We equip them with the skills and strategies to process words, digest language, and generate a response.

> "AS EDUCATORS, WE INVEST A GREAT DEAL OF TIME AND ENERGY IN ENSURING CHILDREN LEARN TO NAVIGATE THE WORDS ON THE PAGE SO THAT THEY CAN DRAW MEANING FROM THE TEXT. WE EQUIP THEM WITH THE SKILLS AND STRATEGIES TO PROCESS WORDS, DIGEST LANGUAGE, AND GENERATE A RESPONSE."

The journey that children take as they travel towards becoming a competent and confident reader can be a long, winding and complex road. So, as well as ensuring that children develop the skills and strategies to lift the words from the page, we must also make sure that they are developing a reader identity and that their reserves are well stocked with the resilience, motivation and enthusiasm necessary for the road ahead. The reading community that we cultivate in our classrooms needs to be underpinned by a learning culture that nourishes and values children's experience, as well as giving them the space to experiment, explore, grow in confidence and develop agency. The key to the success of this community is ensuring that we offer a rich and varied breadth and range of quality literature. Literature that speaks to the children, invites them to make connections with their own and others' lives, and lets them know that they have a place in this reading world. And literature that provides opportunities to discover people and worlds they may not yet know (Cremin et al., 2014).

'The most important single lesson that children learn from texts is *the nature and variety of written discourse*, the different ways that language lets a writer tell, and the different ways a reader reads' (Meek, 1988: 21). Time spent ensuring access to a wide and varied range of literature is therefore crucial to informing and shaping children's knowledge and understanding of language. That said, reflections about what constitutes the breadth and range of literature very quickly become absorbed in considerations about text types. This is of course both valid and important. However, we should also consider what it is that makes a book speak to us, and the extent to which this shapes our book choices and recommendations for the children we work with. By doing this, we are exploring the idea of reader identity and encouraging ourselves to think about how we support children to develop their own identity as a reader and their own literary tastes.

Educators are often the most influential gatekeepers of literature, which means we have a responsibility to ensure that:

- children have access to a broad breadth and range of quality reading materials;
- we are able to draw on our knowledge of our children's interests, personalities and reading preferences, as well as our knowledge of the body of literature on the market, to make considered, discerning and informed recommendations;
- we allow children the time and opportunity to meaningfully engage with reading material. (Chambers, 2011)

In order to be able to develop literary tastes and preferences, children need to experience and encounter a broad range of text types from a wide range of authors, poets and illustrators whose works are representative of varied voices, perspectives, writing styles, literary traditions, contexts, themes, cultures and eras. Such variation is mainly achieved by having access to a large volume of books which of course requires a budget commitment.

The Joseph Rowntree Foundation Annual Poverty Report 2018 forecasts that the upward trend in child poverty over the last few years is likely to continue if urgent action is not taken. The poverty rates cited obviously have a direct effect on disposable income and purchasing power, making the purchasing of books a luxury. This increases the reliance on the school system and public library service to compensate for this, and can mean that for many children in classrooms across England the book corner or school library is their sole source of access to literature. Unfortunately, school budgets are increasingly strained and *The Bookseller* reported in 2018 that spending on the public library service dropped almost 4% in that year compared to the previous year's figures.

Economic forces don't just influence a child's reading diet in relation to how much they consume, they can also shape how balanced and varied that consumption is. If we consider the UK Book Industry in Statistics Report of 2016, produced by the Publisher Association, it is evident that there was at that point a diminishing presence of independent booksellers on the high street. This trend indicates a growing monopolisation of the bookselling market by major online retailers, chains or supermarkets.

This means we have seen an increase in non-specialised booksellers who will show-case stock that will often be limited to a narrow range of bestselling authors. This creates a self-fulfilling cycle of a limited range of literature being on offer on the high street, and that restricted range becoming the default "choice" of children who are able to purchase books.

> "THIS CREATES A SELF-FULFILLING CYCLE OF A LIMITED RANGE OF LITERATURE BEING ON OFFER ON THE HIGH STREET, AND THAT RESTRICTED RANGE BECOMING THE DEFAULT "CHOICE" OF CHILDREN WHO ARE ABLE TO PURCHASE BOOKS."

This is perhaps borne out in Nielsen sales data, which indicates very little movement in the listings of top-selling authors between 2012 and 2017.

In the face of budgetary constraints, socio-economic challenges and the weight of market forces, teachers' role as gatekeepers responsible for ensuring experiences of a rich variation and large volume of quality literature becomes all the more vital.

CONSIDERED RECOMMENDATION

To recommend books effectively we must be well read and knowledgeable about the literature that is available, from well-established titles to the ever-growing contributions made from existing and emerging authors. The UKLA's research on the importance of Teachers as Readers (Cremin et al., 2006–7 and 2007–8) bears testimony to the importance of our knowing books beyond our own childhood favourites. At CLPE, we know from our work with our Power of Reading programme that widening teachers' knowledge of children's literature is a key factor in cultivating a community of readers.

Knowing the books is one thing, knowing which books will speak to our children is another. Through our work with schools around the country, and drawing on our own experience as teachers, we have found that the titles that children tend to make connections with have common features, which include:

- protagonists that children identify with;
- moral dilemmas;
- opportunities to explore risk;
- humour in subject matter, plot, character or dialogue;
- shared experiences.

The importance of connection cannot be overstated, and a core component of connection lies in the opportunity to experience fragments of your own reality reflected in the pages of a book. This 'mirroring' – a term coined by Dr Rudine Sims Bishop (Sims Bishop, 1990) – is a form of affirmation and legitimises the reader's right to occupy the literary space. For young, developing readers this is profoundly important both for their reader and learner identity.

Dr Sims Bishop also discusses the value of texts offering 'windows' into worlds beyond the reader's point of reference. It is just as important for children to experience realities beyond their own in the books they encounter, as this allows opportunities to broaden perspectives, encourage understanding and challenge prejudice.

TEXT CHOICE AND CURRICULUM PLANNING

We know that children who read often and routinely will become competent and confident readers over time. In view of the time constraints and the implications for how many focus texts can form the basis of a class's core study, it is important to choose quality texts that ensure a breadth and balance over the course of the term and more widely across the academic year. Text choices will convey implicit and explicit messages about whose voices and stories are valid and valued. The content and subject matter should allow opportunities to centre a range of voices, perspectives and experiences. By ensuring this, we are able to reinforce the idea that the literary space belongs to us all not only as consumers but also as producers of writing.

A heavily-loaded, subject-focused curriculum will inevitably constrain teachers who are required to ensure coverage. One solution is often to tie in text choices to curriculum study. It is important to think about these choices and to make sure that they neither compromise the quality of text choice nor skew the learning foci towards a narrow, Eurocentric outlook. In the English Programme of Study in the 2013 National Curriculum, the word 'book' is mentioned a total of 71 times across 88 pages. This emphasises the importance of ensuring children experience a broad range of literature over the course of their primary school years, and lists the types of text children should expect to encounter.

When mapping out an overview of potential texts to share and explore as part of your core literacy and wider curriculum planning, it might be useful to keep the following key considerations in mind to ensure that traditionally marginalised voices and narratives form an integral part of your curriculum and wider reading programme.

CONTEMPORARY AND CLASSIC POETRY

Poetry is a powerful medium that allows us to express our thoughts, ideas and emotions. As readers, we bring our world of experience to the page to help us make sense of what we read, as do writers and poets. Therefore the wider the range of poets we encounter, the richer our experience will be.

Do you and your pupils take time to savour and enjoy the poetry of poets from a range of backgrounds? Established poets such as Grace Nichols, Valerie Bloom, John Agard, Jackie Kay and James Berry bring a range of voices to any book corner, as do newer award winning poets such as Karl Nova, Joseph Coelho and Ruth Awolola. More information about the range of poets that can be included in your book stock is available in Chapter 5.

STORIES AND KEY STORIES

The Year 1 Programme of Study detailed in the English National Curriculum states the requirement that children become 'very familiar with key stories, fairy stories and traditional tales, retelling them and considering their particular characteristics' (Department for Education, 2013: 21). It is interesting that the curriculum should use the term 'key' – we might ask key to whom and why? Stories provide a blueprint for our understanding of how language works and narrative structures are formed. Do children have the opportunity to encounter stories that exemplify a wide range of literary styles and perspectives? As well as contemporary Key Stage 1 classroom classics from the likes of Ahlberg, Donaldson, Kerr, Rosen and Sendak, are children experiencing the talents of authors like Atinuke, Emily Hughes, Ken Wilson-Max, and Joseph Coelho, whose works provide authentic inclusive representations of children from a range of backgrounds?

TRADITIONAL STORIES

Traditional stories were crafted to be told and listened to, the rhythms, patterns and structure moulded to be memorable to recount and easy to share and pass on. This type of story should form the bedrock of the primary classroom experience. Given that every culture has their own tradition in this regard, it can sometimes feel like the obvious place to start in terms of broadening access to a wider representation of cultures. This is therefore often the space on the shelf where there is a disproportionately higher level of representation in terms of ethnic minority presence. The study of traditional stories from around the world is a valid and valuable enterprise, however it is always important to reflect on whether this is the only form of story/literature that is studied that features an ethnic minority presence. If this is the case, what might pupils infer about the cultures and societies from which the stories originate? If children only encounter ethnic minorities in stories located in ancient or long-gone eras and in no other reading matter, this might convey the idea that the cultures and societies portrayed have not progressed beyond this point.

MODERN FICTION

If the reading culture of the school is strong, you will have reading routines inside and beyond the classroom that allow for wider experiences of texts. It is in this space that it will be important for children to encounter books in which the ethnicity of the characters are not plot points. Children need to access books in which 'otherness' is not the underpinning feature, and books in which the ethnically inclusive cast are simply living life, having fun, and experiencing every day, sometimes new and often interesting things. In other words, books that allow readers to see themselves and others just existing and co-existing.

Alanna Max Publishers do this exceptionally well. The beautiful, considered attention to detail in both the *Lulu* and *Zeki* picturebook series perfectly captures the simple pleasures of toddler life in an authentic, warm and playful way.

Zanib Mian's award-winning title *The Muslims* that has since been republished under the title *Planet Omar* is being heralded as the next *Diary of a Wimpy Kid*. This comedic take on the life of a young boy who happens to be Muslim is a crucial contribution to the world of children's literature and society. The normalisation of Muslim family life is a much needed and important antidote to the hostile times in which we find ourselves. Sharna Jackson's *High-Rise Mystery* is a fun and lively detective adventure with two young black leads. It is very rare to have ethnic minority leads located in comedy or adventure titles. By making these simple but tremendously important casting choices, both Mian and Jackson are challenging conventions and shifting the narrative by altering the ways in which readers view both themselves and others. For a very long time the only instances in which a reader might encounter an ethnic minority character would be if the subject matter was about struggle, strife, subjugation or success. From exposure to such books a reader might infer that individuals from an ethnic minority background are only worthy of visibility when exploring their points of difference. Furthermore these differences are usually focused on highlighting exceptional qualities that correlate with an exploration of the pain or success of overcoming challenges. If these are the only titles on the shelf featuring characters from minoritised backgrounds, this can lead to limiting and skewed perceptions of whole communities of people.

That is not to say that books that document the successes and struggles of individuals and communities of people are not important. Books like Vashti Harrison's *Little Leaders* series form part of a significant and ever-growing body of literature that celebrates the achievements of inspirational women, and in this case in particular women from minoritised backgrounds. These books are important in exemplifying the best of who we are and what we can achieve. They bear testimony to our core humanity and invaluable attributes of strength, determination and resilience. What is crucial is that we remain mindful of the balance of representation within and across the books we curate for our classrooms and school libraries.

BOOKS FROM OTHER CULTURES AND TRADITIONS

The CLPE Reflecting Realities report highlighted the stark extent of under-representation of ethnic minority presence in children's literature, with only 4% of books published in 2017 featuring black and ethnic minority characters and only 1% of main characters being from ethnic minority backgrounds. We observed only a slight improvement in these figures in the second report that reviewed output from 2018, rising from 4% to 7% and 1% to 4%.

The publishing industry is making efforts to redress this imbalance, but in the interim this can sometimes mean that a greater burden of responsibility can weigh on each title that does make efforts to be authentically representative.

> "THE PUBLISHING INDUSTRY IS MAKING EFFORTS TO REDRESS THIS IMBALANCE, BUT IN THE INTERIM THIS CAN SOMETIMES MEAN THAT A GREATER BURDEN OF RESPONSIBILITY CAN WEIGH ON EACH TITLE THAT DOES MAKE EFFORTS TO BE AUTHENTICALLY REPRESENTATIVE."

One book cannot be expected to be all things for all readers. However when marginalised voices are given a platform the brightness of the spotlight can be blindingly unforgiving. This is why in recommending and sharing books from other cultures and traditions it is important to pick carefully and ensure that your curation is as balanced as possible, and that your book corner showcases the breadth and diversity of experiences of any one community in order to reduce the potential to reinforce stereotypes or convey narrow portrayals.

If we are not mindful in our considerations of which texts to stock and utilise in our classrooms, this can compromise the reading diet and subsequent emerging reader identity of all the children in our care.

As educators, we must consider how limited reading diets can influence children's sense of self and their place in the world.

When making book choices for classrooms, it is always important to consider the balance of your book stock and the extent to which it reflects the reality of the children in your class, your school community and wider society. It is important for the developing identity of all your readers that you ensure a balance and breadth of quality, inclusion and representation.

We are all made up of the stories that we tell ourselves, that have been told to us and about us. Who we are and who we become as individuals and a society is bound up in the fabric of these stories. As gatekeepers of the literature, teachers have a responsibility to nurture the readers of tomorrow through the stories we share today.

REFERENCES

Chambers, A. (2011) *Tell Me: Children, Reading & Talk with The Reading Environment*. Stroud: Thimble Press.

CLPE (2018) *Reflecting Realities: Survey of Ethnic Representation within UK Children's Literature 2017*. London: CLPE.

CLPE (2019) *Reflecting Realities: Survey of Ethnic Representation within UK Children's Literature 2018*. London: CLPE.

Cremin, T., Bearne, E., Mottram, M. and Goodwin, P. (2006-7) Teachers as Readers: Phase 1 Research Report for UKLA.

Cremin, T., Mottram, M., Collins, F.M., Powell, S. and Safford, K. (2007–8) Teachers as Readers: Building Communities of Readers Phase 2 Research Report for UKLA.

Cremin, T., Mottram, M., Collins, F.M., Powell, S. and Safford, K. (2014) *Building Communities of Readers: Reading for Pleasure*. Abingdon: Routledge.

Department for Education (2013) The National Curriculum in England Key Stages 1 and 2 Framework Document. London: DfE.

Joseph Rowntree Foundation Annual Poverty Report 2018 – www.jrf.org.uk/report/uk-poverty-2018

Meek, M. (1988) *How Texts Teach What Readers Learn*. Stroud: Thimble Press.

Page, B. (2018) Latest CIPFA Stats Reveal Yet More Library Closures and Book Loan Falls, *Bookseller* Article – https://www.thebookseller.com/news/cipfa-records-yet-more-library-closures-and-book-loan-falls-911061

Publishers Association – www.publishers.org.uk/

Sims Bishop, R. (1990) 'Mirrors, windows and sliding glass doors', *Perspectives: Choosing and Using Books for the Classroom, 6* (3).

CHILDREN'S BOOKS REFERENCED IN THIS CHAPTER

Harrison, V. (2018) *Little Leaders: Bold Women in Black History*. London: Puffin.

Harrison, V. (2018) *Little Leaders: Visionary Women Around the World*. London: Puffin.

Jackson, S. (2019) *High-Rise Mystery*. Brixton: Knights Of.

McQuinn, A. (Author) Beardshaw, R. (Illustrator) (2019) *Lulu's First Day*. London: Alanna Max.

McQuinn, A. (Author) Beardshaw, R. (Illustrator) (2017) *Lulu Gets a Cat*. London: Alanna Max.

McQuinn, A. (Author) Beardshaw, R. (Illustrator) (2009) *Lulu Loves the Library*. London: Alanna Max.

McQuinn, A. (Author) Beardshaw, R. (Illustrator) (2016) *Lulu Loves Flowers*. London: Alanna Max.

McQuinn, A. (Author) Beardshaw, R. (Illustrator) (2011) *Lulu Loves Stories*. London: Alanna Max.

McQuinn, A. (Author) Beardshaw, R. (Illustrator) (2011) *Lulu Reads to Zeki*. London: Alanna Max.

McQuinn, A. (Author) Beardshaw, R. (Illustrator) (2018) *Zeki Gets a Checkup*. London: Alanna Max.

McQuinn, A. (Author) Beardshaw, R. (Illustrator) (2016) *Zeki Can Swim!* London: Alanna Max.

McQuinn, A. (Author) Beardshaw, R. (Illustrator) (2014) *Zeki Loves Baby Club*. London: Alanna Max.

Mian, Z. (Author) Mafaridik, N. (Illustrator) (2019) *Accidental Trouble Magnet: Book 1 (Planet Omar)*. London: Hodder Children's Books.

CHAPTER 2

CHOOSING AND USING TEXTS FOR EARLY READERS: WHY IT MATTERS

ANJALI PATEL

Being part of a child's reading journey from the very earliest stages is one of life's joys. Teaching children to read for purpose and pleasure is possibly the most important job of all. Reading is the foundation on which being literate stands and it is every child's entitlement to be literate. Being literate gives children voice, enables social inclusion and literally increases life chances (Literacy Trust, 2018).

Firstly, we need to acknowledge the complexities involved in learning to read. As much as we may want to simplify the process – perhaps in the hope of making it more accessible – teaching reading can't be reduced to a single approach. It does require subject knowledge to do it well, i.e. knowledge of reading development, knowledge of texts, and crucially, knowledge of each child you want to teach.

Each child comes with their own reading experiences, identity, knowledge and skills that we can build on to teach reading. Observing early readers and knowing what questions to ask about them is crucial.

"EACH CHILD COMES WITH THEIR OWN READING EXPERIENCES, IDENTITY, KNOWLEDGE AND SKILLS THAT WE CAN BUILD ON TO TEACH READING. OBSERVING EARLY READERS AND KNOWING WHAT QUESTIONS TO ASK ABOUT THEM IS CRUCIAL."

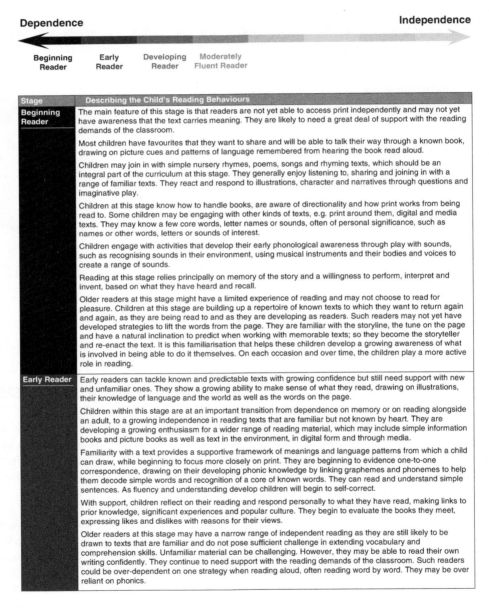

Dependence

Independence

Beginning Reader | Early Reader | Developing Reader | Moderately Fluent Reader

Stage	Describing the Child's Reading Behaviours
Beginning Reader	The main feature of this stage is that readers are not yet able to access print independently and may not yet have awareness that the text carries meaning. They are likely to need a great deal of support with the reading demands of the classroom.
	Most children have favourites that they want to share and will be able to talk their way through a known book, drawing on picture cues and patterns of language remembered from hearing the book read aloud.
	Children may join in with simple nursery rhymes, poems, songs and rhyming texts, which should be an integral part of the curriculum at this stage. They generally enjoy listening to, sharing and joining in with a range of familiar texts. They react and respond to illustrations, character and narratives through questions and imaginative play.
	Children at this stage know how to handle books, are aware of directionality and how print works from being read to. Some children may be engaging with other kinds of texts, e.g. print around them, digital and media texts. They may know a few core words, letter names or sounds, often of personal significance, such as names or other words, letters or sounds of interest.
	Children engage with activities that develop their early phonological awareness through play with sounds, such as recognising sounds in their environment, using musical instruments and their bodies and voices to create a range of sounds.
	Reading at this stage relies principally on memory of the story and a willingness to perform, interpret and invent, based on what they have heard and recall.
	Older readers at this stage might have a limited experience of reading and may not choose to read for pleasure. Children at this stage are building up a repertoire of known texts to which they want to return again and again, as they are being read to and as they are developing as readers. Such readers may not yet have developed strategies to lift the words from the page. They are familiar with the storyline, the tune on the page and have a natural inclination to predict when working with memorable texts; so they become the storyteller and re-enact the text. It is this familiarisation that helps these children develop a growing awareness of what is involved in being able to do it themselves. On each occasion and over time, the children play a more active role in reading.
Early Reader	Early readers can tackle known and predictable texts with growing confidence but still need support with new and unfamiliar ones. They show a growing ability to make sense of what they read, drawing on illustrations, their knowledge of language and the world as well as the words on the page.
	Children within this stage are at an important transition from dependence on memory or on reading alongside an adult, to a growing independence in reading texts that are familiar but not known by heart. They are developing a growing enthusiasm for a wider range of reading material, which may include simple information books and picture books as well as text in the environment, in digital form and through media.
	Familiarity with a text provides a supportive framework of meanings and language patterns from which a child can draw, while beginning to focus more closely on print. They are beginning to evidence one-to-one correspondence, drawing on their developing phonic knowledge by linking graphemes and phonemes to help them decode simple words and recognition of a core of known words. They can read and understand simple sentences. As fluency and understanding develop children will begin to self-correct.
	With support, children reflect on their reading and respond personally to what they have read, making links to prior knowledge, significant experiences and popular culture. They begin to evaluate the books they meet, expressing likes and dislikes with reasons for their views.
	Older readers at this stage may have a narrow range of independent reading as they are still likely to be drawn to texts that are familiar and do not pose sufficient challenge in extending vocabulary and comprehension skills. Unfamiliar material can be challenging. However, they may be able to read their own writing confidently. They continue to need support with the reading demands of the classroom. Such readers could be over-dependent on one strategy when reading aloud, often reading word by word. They may be over reliant on phonics.

Figure 2.1

Whilst every child's reading journey is unique, there are behaviours common in most early readers that we can look out for. The CLPE Reading Scale (2016) describes the progression through the complex process of learning to read. It offers teachers a description of reading behaviours at each stage of the learning to read journey. Different children will have a varied and broad range of starting points and experience and the route of their individual progress will very much depend on this prior experience. The Scales are a free resource and useful to look at if you are unsure about the key characteristics of beginner and early readers.

This chapter will focus primarily on choosing and using texts that will enable you to develop in early readers the attitudes, skills and knowledge when teaching reading in the Early Years, but also discusses older early readers as specific considerations need to be made when meeting their needs.

KEY THINGS TO CONSIDER WITH EARLY READERS

One of the first things to reflect upon when working with early readers is the influence we have on their perceptions of reading. How do they view reading itself? What does it involve? And do they consider themselves to be a reader? These questions and their potential responses rely on the provision we put in place, the texts we draw upon, and the language we use with children and their families. So how do we achieve a balance so that we can build on experiences, share knowledge, teach key skills and strategies, and develop positive attitudes in children towards reading and reader identity in themselves?

Children who have had a good balance of sharing high-quality texts with enthusiastic adults whilst simultaneously being encouraged to take an interest in, and tune in to, the print itself are more likely to want to read. Reading takes practice and needs stamina, and this relies on maintaining children's interest and self-esteem at the early stages of reading. We need to harness their drive to find meaning in print and this is easier when what is being read has greater significance for them. We also need to ensure that every child has access to a wide range of texts at home and at school to help establish their regular enjoyment of reading, foster positive attitudes and allow for the development of reader identity within a community of readers.

To achieve this we need to work towards creating a classroom which is infused by story, rhyme and song; where reading happens alone, is shared with friends and is guided by trusted adults; in which stories are retold, re-enacted and reimagined through talk and play; in which every child sees themselves as a reader.

Sharing stories with strong characterisation, memorable language and linear narratives lends itself well to role play and re-enactment. Who can imagine reading Michael Rosen's *We're Going on a Bear Hunt* with children without them being active participants throughout? When children look at Helen Oxenbury's illustration of the bear walking away in the end papers, it will provoke an affective response, allowing them to draw on their experience of human relationships and behaviour – just as when you read aloud, in a pathetic voice, baby Bill's refrain "I want my mummy", from Martin Waddell's and Patrick Benson's *Owl Babies*. And when you share Pat Huchin's *Rosie's Walk* with children, they will hear the text you read but be absorbed by the storyline playing out in the illustrations.

When children are reading pictures in this way, they are demonstrating sophisticated visual literacy and reading behaviours.

Nursery rhymes will often be children's first experience of fictional narrative as well as providing strong tunes, rhyming structures and sing-a-long actions that support memorisation. Children enjoy joining in with nursery rhymes on screen as a kind of karaoke activity, and a book of rhymes and verse like *The Oxford Book of Nursery Rhymes* in your book area will allow children to return to the print version independently.

Texts with memorable rhymes and patterned language, including traditional tales, will help children develop an 'ear' for language. Making sure that you have a core collection of well-known, favourite books will allow children to participate in the reading experience and provide a sense of what fluent reading is. Practising this behaviour allows children to see themselves as readers. Julia Donaldon and Axel Sheffler's *The Gruffalo* is an enduring classic because it is so enjoyable to share with children. Once captivated by the characters and story, even the smallest children can chime in and then feel as though they are reading this book independently, drawing on their memory of refrain, strong tunes and rhyming patterns.

Valuing children's popular culture, their home languages and literacies can also include comics and texts in home languages in reading areas as well as props in the role play area that show languages other than English. Invite parents into the setting to read stories and sing songs in their own languages or to contribute to a collection of audio recordings. The relationship between school and home reading is particularly important for early readers. Supporting the families of children in our classrooms to borrow books and feel confident and knowledgeable enough to build reading routines at home is a key part of a classroom where early readers thrive.

Building a reading environment that supports children's reading journey means ensuring the book stock offers a range of engaging reading experiences – a breadth and range of texts that will encourage children to browse and make text choice of stories, poetry, rhyme, comics and information texts. Include books that spark personal interest that will motivate children to read, as well as offering an opportunity to teach and practise specific reading strategies and behaviours.

Through all of these classroom routines and experiences we can build a range of opportunities where children are encouraged to read a wide range of texts and to see themselves as readers and reading as pleasurable activity. Learning to read is a complex human process and we need to make sure that teaching reading isn't reduced to just one strategy. Emergent reading is never left to chance. We plan for it and nurture it through carefully crafted experiences and with a range of engaging and enabling quality texts.

KEY FEATURES OF TEXTS THAT SUPPORT EARLY READERS

Rich reading routines and experiences to support children's positive attitudes to reading and their reader identity will underpin their developing knowledge and skills in both decoding and comprehension.

It is important to keep a regular read aloud programme when children start independent print reading and decoding, because it is through this that you can ᴄ... ...¸ comprehension and response to texts that take them beyond what they can read and understand independently; rich texts and illustration that support children to reflect on their own reading and to respond in a range of ways, to make personal connections, ask questions, summarise and developing inference and deeper understanding.

Carefully planned stopping points when reading aloud support children's developing critical literacy further. In *Owl Babies* children can be encouraged to make connections with their personal experiences as well as other stories they know. They can ask questions about how the owls feel surrounded by the dark woodland; whether we think Sophie is as brave as she appears and what this tells us about her character and her relationship with her siblings; why mum has to leave the baby owls at all.

Shared reading enables you to demonstrate the strategies involved in independent print reading. Choose books with supportive features that allow a demonstration of reading strategies and opportunities to draw on a balance of reading cues: strong tunes; patterned language such as repeated refrain, rhyme and analogy, onset and rime; predictable sentence structures; decodable words or elements of; known words; meaningful vocabulary; illustrations that work with the text to support meaning. When reading aloud familiar rhymes and stories like *The Gruffalo*, you can enlarge the print and increase their sensitivity to it by pointing out directionality and one-to-one correspondence so that when children read for themselves through memorisation it will become apparent to them if they run out of printed words, for example. You can show them how punctuation works given that reading aloud is a kind of performance. Books like Ed Vere's *Banana!* provide the perfect experience of this in action as little is said other than 'banana', but the picture cues and the punctuation work together in harmony to make meaning for the reader. There are a great many books that will help you support children's developing phonological awareness in enriching ways. Reading *Lullabyhullaballoo* by Mick Inkpen with children provides much enjoyment and scope for increasing their awareness of the plentiful environmental sounds around the castle that are keeping the little princess awake. The lift-the-flap pages reveal the source of the disturbance and to the sound being made, cleverly represented by words in the speech bubbles, drawing attention to the print. Even without being able to decode, children will begin to notice sound and spelling patterns as they become more familiar with each page. Later, when children learn to blend and segment consonant clusters, these onomatopoeic words will create a meaningful context ('CLUNK, CLANK').

Stories that involve a journey through contrasting settings, such as *Bedtime for Monsters* by Ed Vere, or those that have shifts in a character's emotional journey, such as *Iris and Isaac* by Catherine Rayner, lend themselves well to activities where children create soundscapes. This supports them to compare the instrumental sounds in terms of pitch and dynamics as you might when reading aloud, as well as preparing children to access the alphabetic code.

"BOOKS THAT HELP CHILDREN TO UNDERSTAND AND ARTICULATE SOUNDS WILL HELP THEM PRACTISE AND EXPRESS THE VARIETY OF SOUNDS THEY ARE LIKELY TO ENCOUNTER WHEN LEARNING THE PHONEMES IN THE ALPHABETIC CODE."

Books that help children to understand and articulate sounds will help them practise and express the variety of sounds they are likely to encounter when learning the phonemes in the alphabetic code (long, short, unvoiced). *What the Ladybird Heard* by Julia Donaldson and Lydia Monks enables children to draw on their familiarity with the sounds of Old MacDonald's farm animals, when re-enacting this exciting tale of trickery in which the animals make sounds belonging to another animal to foil the robber's dastardly plan. By making plans and maps to emulate the Ladybird's, the children can be encouraged to write their new sound in speech bubbles, paying attention to the print in an enjoyable context and reinforcing the relationship between talk, writing and reading.

Children also need to practise the vocabulary to describe the sounds they hear and say. In *Polar Bear, Polar Bear, What Can You Hear?* Eric Carle has gifted us with glorious refrains like 'I hear a flamingo fluting in my ear', thereby introducing children to uplifting language that they might not encounter in everyday conversations.

By hearing, reading and performing poetry, children begin to develop an appreciation of the sound patterns within words. The inclusion of a range of accessible, shareable and learnable poetry within classroom collections is so important for children who are learning to read and later to spell. Michael Rosen's gift for word play is epitomised in *A Great Big Cuddle*, leaving readers young and old with the infectious need to enjoy and explore language – the way it sounds, the way it feels in the mouth, and the way it looks in print. The poems vary in rhythmic pattern and children enjoy performing them, using body percussion to play with a syllabic beat and lifting meaning from the page with actions, vocalisation and instrumental effects.

Once the foundations of early phonological awareness are in place, attitudes to reading are positive and reader identity is strong, children can begin to build on this to start to pay closer attention to the letter sound correspondences, and will be able to learn phonics in a systematic and enjoyable way. This should be seen as a continuation of a child's reading journey through rich reading experiences and using quality texts alongside decodable texts to provide authentic contexts to read and write independently.

The Cat Sat on the Mat by Brian Wildsmith challenges us to define the archetype of 'a simple text'. The repetitive sentences are simple in structure and almost totally decodable for children at the early stages of learning the basic code involving single letter-sound corre-spondence and high-frequency whole words. The illustrations indeed support the text, enabling an early reader to walk through the book with an adult to anticipate what the text may say as well as using picture cues to read animal names such as 'elephant' with fluency. However, they do much more than that. The cow may very well sit on the mat but it doesn't mean the cat has to be happy about this.

The scope for deeper responses in this deceptively simple text is marvellous and it demands to be discussed and re-read. Wildsmith's book and others like it, such as *I am in a Book* from the Ellie and Piggie series by Mo Willems, enable children to practise their reading and sends the message that, even though they are having to work quite hard at reading for themselves now, they can draw on what they know about reading and – most importantly – it will be worthwhile and enjoyable. This is the stuff of nurturing lifelong readers.

KEY FEATURES OF TEXTS THAT SUPPORT OLDER EARLY READERS

Older children identified as early readers need to be really closely observed and monitored. There will be no one-size-fits-all option. We need to take the time to find out about and develop older children's reader identity, providing access to texts that will motivate them to read for purpose and pleasure and promote inclusion in the class reading community. Part of this will be to provide reading routines and texts that provide an opportunity to experience a greater variety of reading material and styles of reading across the curriculum. The texts chosen should support the modelling and consolidation of reading skills and strategies but also reflect children's strengths, interests, cultures and reading preferences, such as:

- books with themes that meet the children's emotional and intellectual needs and in a style appropriate to the children's age and experience, such as *Grandpa Green* by Lane Smith, *The Day of Ahmed's Secret* by Florence Parry Heide, or *The Stepsister's Story* by Kaye Umansky;
- books that develop visual and emotional literacy alongside print reading, like Anthony Browne's *Voices in the Park* or *The Dam* by David Almond and Levi Pinfold;
- familiar texts like *Angry Arthur* by Kitamura or *Green Eggs and Ham* by Dr Seuss that support children in risk-taking and reading aloud and independently;
- carefully chosen less well-known texts that have supportive features, that encourage reading stamina and fluency with engaging storylines and strong tunes, and those that can be read and revisited alongside a more experienced reader in relaxed enjoyable ways, such as *The Fish Who Could Wish* by John Bush and Korky Paul and *Yo! Yes?* by Chris Raschka;
- texts like *Is There a Dog in This Book?* by Viviane Schwarz or *Du Iz Tak* by Carsen and Ellis, that enable children to reflect on their reading strategies and allow the opportunity to learn to orchestrate a wider range of reading cues;
- poetry that encourages an interest in words and developing a repertoire of vocabulary with which they can make connections to visual spelling patterns, relying less on the phonemic qualities of a word, like Michael Rosen's *Mustard, Custard, Grumble, Belly and Gravy* or Grace Nichol's *Cosmic Disco*.

PROVISION FOR EARLY READERS WHO ARE EXPERIENCING DIFFERENT TYPES OF DIFFICULTY

Factors affecting children with reading difficulties are extremely diverse, vary enormously from child to child, and may include physiological, medical, sensory, emotional, and social factors as well as a whole number of issues such as home and school environment, motivation and learning preferences. Similarly, provision to meet children's needs must take into account all of these, and should be based on the concept that learning to read is a complex orchestration of many different skills. Rather than generalising, we need to establish what children can do and build on this with carefully planned experiences around engaging texts.

Most children will depend on either print or meaning strategies in the early stages of reading as they develop the ability to orchestrate the various aspects of the reading process. Occasionally, however, they may become stuck and continue to depend on either print cues or meaning cues. They may then need support to move along. This does not necessarily imply specialised or separate activities. Some activities like bookmaking are valuable for all children and every child needs to be motivated by the reading material. Nonetheless, there are some strategies and text types that can be particularly supportive for certain older early readers.

Slow to begin reading

- Books in which the matching of voice and word can become very explicit.
- Books that read aloud well and through which we can model reading behaviours such as finger and voice pointing during their reading.
- Books that inspire shared writing in small groups where the features of print-directionality, words, spaces, letters and names, as well as issues like rhyme and repetition, can be focused on.
- Opportunities to dictate and make into books their own stories, especially their own re-tellings of favourite books and well-known stories.
- We can use children's names, family and class names, sweet labels and cartoon characters to make books that can help to develop their awareness of print. Children can tick off their own class register on a daily basis.
- Books, songs, poems and rhymes – from nursery rhymes to advertising jingles and pop songs – can be made into books for sharing.

Overdependent on print cues

Readers in this group depend mainly on decoding strategies, and fail to realise that they can use their knowledge of the story, context, or language to predict words. Older readers of this type may have become reliant on 'scheme' books of the type in which decoding has been the major method of reading. Children may predict wildly, based on the look of words, and carry on despite the fact that the text no longer makes sense to them. Such children can be helped to develop their reading as follows:

- Using shared book writing to develop understanding of how books and language work. Beginner writers can dictate their books and stories to an adult.
- Listening and re-listening to favourite books and stories, ensuring those with strong, rhythmic and lively texts are strongly represented. Audio books are useful to allow older children to join in with stories in situations without being too exposed.
- Careful choice of texts which are most meaningful to better enable children to make sense of their reading.
- Cloze-type activities, such as blanking out the words in a text and encouraging predictions based on the context.
- A child's own books and stories can be photocopied and then cut up into chunks and reassembled so that they develop an overview of a particular story.

Overdependent on meaning cues

These children may find it difficult to attend to print cues, using mainly their memory for books, stories and language to support their reading. Strategies which help to focus attention on print are as follows:

- Shared reading of books, including the modelling of finger and voice pointing, using strong rhythmic texts where it is easy to match voice to word.
- Shared writing where all the features of print letters, words and punctuation together with sound/letter correspondences can be made explicit.

- Cloze-type activities which use the first and possibly other letters as cues.
- Writing their own books and stories and using these for reading material inevitably focuses attention on print in very important ways. Composing and typing up their own writing on a computer further reinforces ideas about print.
- The use of word and letter games, e.g. I Spy and Snap games using objects which begin with the same letter/sound.

Being a Primary School teacher is being a teacher of reading. Arguably, there is little else that matters more in a child's educational journey. Reading independently and for pleasure is the key to educational success in all areas of the curriculum, as it allows children to live longer and leads to a richer life lived.

"BEING A PRIMARY SCHOOL TEACHER IS BEING A TEACHER OF READING. ARGUABLY, THERE IS LITTLE ELSE THAT MATTERS MORE IN A CHILD'S EDUCATIONAL JOURNEY. READING INDEPENDENTLY AND FOR PLEASURE IS THE KEY TO EDUCATIONAL SUCCESS IN ALL AREAS OF THE CURRICULUM, AS IT ALLOWS CHILDREN TO LIVE LONGER AND IT LEADS TO A RICHER LIFE LIVED."

Understanding the complexities of learning to read is about respecting the unique nature of each child and embracing the breadth of reading experiences you want them to access. Being literate depends on a successful start in decoding print alongside – not instead of – a continuing drive to engage in reading quality texts that build on interests, child development and a foundation of rich reading routines. Understanding this allows us to unpick the provision we have in place for our early readers, i.e. the books we choose to support our knowledge of reading progression but that also reflect each of our reader's experience, identity, needs and interests.

As Cathy Nutbrown says 'if we can light the flame of the love of literature' (Nutbrown, 1994: 92) from the start, we are likely to raise a generation of devoted readers.

REFERENCES

CLPE (2016) *The Reading Scale*. London: CLPE.
CLPE (1991) *The Reading Book*. London: CLPE.
Literacy Trust (2018) *Literacy and Life Expectancy*. London: Literacy Trust.
Nutbrown, C. (1994) *Threads of Thinking: Schemas and Young Children's Learning*. London: Sage.

RESOURCES

CLPE (2016) *The Reading Scale* https://clpe.org.uk/library-and-resources/reading-and-writing-scales
CLPE (2018) *What We Know Works: Choosing and Using Quality Texts* https://clpe.org.uk/library-and-resources/what-we-know-works-booklets/choosing-and-using-quality-childrens-texts-what-we

Core Books https://clpe.org.uk/corebooks
CLPE Power of Reading website https://clpe.org.uk/powerofreading

FiND OUT MORE

Sullivan, A. and Brown, M. (2015) Reading for pleasure and progress in vocabulary and mathematics. *British Educational Research Journal*, 41(6).

Dombey, H., Moustafa, M. and CLPE Staff (1998) *Whole to Part Phonics: How Children Learn to Read and Spell*. London: CLPE.

Castles, A., Rastle, K. and Nation, K. (2018) *Ending the Reading Wars: Reading Acquisition from Novice to Expert*. Sage.pub.com

Clark, M. et al. (2017) *Reading the Evidence: Synthetic Phonics and Literacy Learning*. Birmingham: Glendale Education.

Clay, M. (2015) *Becoming Literate*. New York: Scholastic.

CLPE (1991) *The Reading Book*. London: CLPE.

Gooch, K. and Lambirth, A. (2007) *Understanding Phonics and the Teaching of Reading*. Oxford: OUP.

Goswami, U. and Bryant, P. (2016) *Phonological Skills and Learning to Read*. Abingdon: Routledge.

Graham, J. and Kelly, A. (2010) *Reading Under Control: Teaching Reading in the Primary School*. Abingdon: Routledge.

Meek, M. (1986) *Learning to Read*. London: Bodley Head.

Richmond, J. (2015) *English, Language and Literacy 3-19 - Principles: Reading 3-7 and 7-16*, UKLA and Owen Education.

Torgerson, C., Brooks, G. and Hall, J. (2006) *A Systematic Review of the Research Literature on the Use of Phonics in the Teaching of Reading and Writing*, Core.ac.uk

CHiLDREN'S BOOKS REFERENCED iN THiS CHAPTER

Almond, D. and Pinfold, L. (2018) *The Dam*. London: Walker.

Browne, A. (1999) *Voices in the Park*. London: Corgi Books.

Bush, J. and Paul, K. (2008) *The Fish Who Could Wish*. Oxford: OUP.

Carle, E. (2007) *Polar Bear, Polar Bear, What Do You Hear?* London: Puffin.

Donaldson, J. and Sheffler, A. (2017) *The Gruffalo*. Basingstoke: Macmillan.

Donaldson, J. and Monks, L. (2010) *What the Ladybird Heard*. Basingstoke: Macmillan.

Dr Seuss (2016) *Green Eggs and Ham*. New York: HarperCollins Children's Books.

Ellis, C. (2017) *Du Iz Tak*. London: Walker.

Heide, P. Heide Gililand, F. and Lewin, T. (1997)*The Day of Ahmed's Secret*. London: Pufffin.

Huchins, P. (2009) *Rosie's Walk*. London: Red Fox Picture Books.

Inkpen, M. (2017) *A Royal Lullabyhullaballoo*. London: Hodder Children's Books.

King, K., Williams, S. and Beck, I. (2014) *The Oxford Treasury of Nursery Rhymes*. Oxford: OUP.

Nichol, G. (2013) *Cosmic Disco*. London: Frances Lincoln.

Oram, H. and Kitamura, S. (2008. *Angry Arthur*. London: Anderson.

Raschka, C. (2007) *Yo! Yes?* New York: Scholastic.

Rayner, C. (2011) *Iris and Isaac*. London: Little Tiger Press.

Rosen, M. and Blake, Q. (2007) *Mustard, Custard, Grumble, Belly and Gravy*. London: Bloomsbury.

Rosen, M. and Oxenbury, H. (1993) *We're Going on a Bear Hunt*. London: Walker.

Rosen, M. and Riddell, C. (2015) *A Great Big Cuddle*. London: Walker.

Schwarz, V. (2015) *Is There a Dog in this Book?* London: Walker.

Smith, L. (2017) *Grandpa Green*. London: Two Hoots.

Umansky, K. (2012) *The Stepsisters' Story*. Edinburgh: Barrington Stoke.

Vere, E. (2007) *Banana!* London: Puffin.

Vere, E. (2011) *Bedtime for Monsters*. London: Puffin.

Waddell, M. and Benson, P. (1994) *Owl Babies*. London: Walker.

Wildsmith, B. (1982) *The Cat Sat on the Mat*. Oxford: OUP.

Willems, M. (2010) *I am in a Book* (Elephant and Piggie Books). New York: Hyperion Books for Children.

CHAPTER 3

FICTION TEXTS IN THE PRIMARY SCHOOL

ANN LAZIM

In this chapter the significance of story in children's lives and education is highlighted. Criteria that teachers need to consider in selecting fiction for their classroom collections and school libraries are outlined. A variety of examples of classic and current children's fiction are introduced, covering a range of genres, with a particular emphasis on traditional stories which form the bedrock of storytelling in all its forms.

THE IMPORTANCE OF FICTION

Stories have always been essential to human thinking. We seek patterns from which to make meaning and understand the world. This need for narrative has been described as 'a primary act of mind' (Hardy, 1977: 12–23).

From the outset, children need to encounter meaningful, memorable and rewarding texts. They need stories that both reflect their own lives *and* that take them to places and times they may never otherwise visit and enable their imaginations to soar.

"FROM THE OUTSET, CHILDREN NEED TO ENCOUNTER MEANINGFUL, MEMORABLE AND REWARDING TEXTS. THEY NEED STORIES THAT BOTH REFLECT THEIR OWN LIVES *AND* THAT TAKE THEM TO PLACES AND TIMES THEY MAY NEVER OTHERWISE VISIT AND ENABLE THEIR IMAGINATIONS TO SOAR."

Not only does this increase knowledge, it also enables empathy with other human beings and with the natural world, as well as a greater understanding of their own emotions (Rosenblatt, 1978; O'Sullivan & McGonigle, 2010; Chiaet, 2013; Hammond, 2019). Reading fiction increases vocabulary, introducing words in context and a much wider range than are used in everyday speech (Cunningham & Stanovich, 1998; Krashen, 2004; Smith, 2012).

A rich reading diet will include a range of texts, in format and in subject matter and genre and in a variety of voices. Fiction encompasses a wide range of forms – picturebooks (discussed in a separate chapter with selected examples referred to here), novels, short stories and traditional tales. Illustration may play a part in any of these. Genres can include historical, animal stories, detective, science fiction, fantasy, contemporary and humorous stories. Children's early encounters with different genres will develop their tastes and may influence what they choose to read as adults. Many books will not fit exclusively into a genre and may cross over between more than one or not fit into any. Humour is an important element in children's fiction – they will frequently ask for a funny book. And also often for a scary one!

As teachers and librarians we need to build our own knowledge of children's fiction so that we can recommend the right book for the right child at the right time and help them broaden their reading range. We also need to listen to what children already know and respect their choices, for example books in popular series. These texts can draw children into the world of reading, provide reading practice, and encourage them to read for pleasure. As Neil Gaiman, an author who draws on many references to literary and popular culture in his own fiction for children and adults, said: "Well-meaning adults can easily destroy a child's love of reading: stop them reading what they enjoy, or give them worthy-but-dull books that you like, the 21st Century equivalents of Victorian 'improving' literature. You'll wind up with a generation convinced that reading is uncool and worse, unpleasant" (Gaiman, 2013).

THE KEY FEATURES OF A GOOD FICTION TEXT

If you are choosing fiction for your classroom you will want to be thinking about a range of texts. You will want to include books that can form the basis of a literature curriculum and introduce children to a growing range of texts. Whilst some children in the class may not be able to read all the books independently, an important function of any collection will be to give them access to a wider range of titles, authors and genres than they might otherwise meet. For more experienced readers, you will want to offer an increasingly challenging range of material for individual or group reading. You will want to ensure you have a range of fiction within your classroom collections and include:

- texts that are multi-layered, capable of being read at different levels;
- books that deal with important themes;

- books in which language is used in lively, inventive ways;
- books in which characters are well developed to encourage empathy;
- books by skilful and experienced children's writers and illustrators;
- traditional and contemporary 'classics' of children's literature;
- stories with different cultural settings and reference points;
- fiction that reflects the backgrounds and realities of the children in your class, and in our wider world;
- texts that promote discussion and reflection.

For a book to be suitable as a class text, around which teachers and children can develop discussion, writing and creative work, it needs to be worth revisiting. It should inspire thinking and creativity, provoke questions, and lead to learning opportunities across the curriculum.

"SHARING BOOKS WITH CHILDREN BY READING ALOUD IS VITAL AS IT WILL ENABLE THEM TO HAVE ACCESS TO LANGUAGE AND STORIES THAT THEY MAY NOT YET BE ABLE TO READ FOR THEMSELVES. IMPORTANTLY IT ALSO ALLOWS CHILDREN TO BECOME PART OF A COMMUNITY OF READERS WHO HAVE ALL BEEN ABLE TO SHARE THE SAME TEXT."

Sharing books with children by reading aloud is vital as it will enable them to have access to language and stories that they may not yet be able to read for themselves. Importantly it also allows children to become part of a community of readers who have all been able to share the same text. Therefore, choosing books that read aloud well is a significant element of book selection.

TRADITIONAL TALES

Ever since people began telling each other stories and an oral tradition evolved, story structures have emerged. Not simply the idea of a beginning, a middle and an end, but clear patterns which readers will recognise as they become familiar with them. Traditional tales include a wide range of narratives – myths and legends, fables, folk and fairy tales. These stories represent the roots of literature – the place where the oral story and the literature in books meet. The patterns and structures of myths and legends, folk and fairy tales underlie and link to much modern fiction for children and for adults. These links may be obvious, such as the Russian Baba Yaga character who inhabits Sophie Anderson's *The House with Chicken Legs*, or more subtle to tease out, such as the Norse gods that appear in modern clothes in *Eight Days of Luke* by Diana Wynne Jones. Therefore, it is vital to have a range of these stories in any classroom and school library, and they need to form part of any reading aloud programme.

Between Worlds by Kevin Crossley-Holland is a collection of stories from around Britain and Ireland retold by a writer steeped in folk and fairy tales, myths and legends, who interprets these for a modern audience while paying respectful attention to the rich flavour of the language in which they were recorded. In compiling her *Fairy Tales* collection, mostly taken from the Western European tradition, Berlie Doherty has used several sources and shaped her own retellings. Her comment that 'Even the most familiar stories have echoes in many different cultures around the world' is reflected in Jane Ray's sumptuous illustrations which frame every page, as she portrays the characters with a variety of skin hues. Carol Ann Duffy uses colloquial everyday language for many of her retellings in *Faery Tales*, making them great to read aloud and harking back to the oral tradition from whence many of them came. Lots of the stories emanate from the Brothers Grimm but there are also nods to literary French tales and Hans Christian Andersen, and some of her own stories drawing on fairy tale elements are also included. Jamila Gavin has fashioned her own set of fairy tales in *Blackberry Blue*, drawing principally on the European traditions with which she grew up. With the expressed aim of increased inclusivity, she has created characters who are people of colour.

Traditional tales can be used in introducing children to a diverse range of cultures at the same time as helping them understand that many similar stories appear across the world. However, there is a lack of diversity in what is published in terms of traditional tales from across the globe although there is a wider range than in fiction with modern contemporary settings. Examples include Madhur Jaffrey's collection of Indian folk tales, *Seasons of Splendour*, in which she recalls the rich storytelling traditions of her own childhood in Delhi, and *African Tales*, in which renowned South African storyteller Gcina Mhlophe retells traditional stories from the length and breadth of Africa.

Many teachers have found that Marcia Williams' comic strip approach to Greek mythology in *Greek Myths* and *The Iliad and the Odyssey* has stimulated children's own writing and led to further exploration of these important stories. In the 'Twelve Tasks of Heracles' the comic strip medium is shown to particular advantage – the tasks are described in the text and the way Heracles tackles them is shown in the pictures. In *Adventures of Odysseus*, storytellers Hugh Lupton and Daniel Morden adapt their oral retelling of this epic. Framed by the story of Penelope and her long wait for the return of her husband, we hear the gory tale of one-eyed Cyclops, marvel at Circe's ability to change men into pigs, and are moved by Odysseus's reunion with his son. The narrative shifts between the third person and Odysseus's own voice, giving immediacy to the telling.

In Michael Morpurgo's retelling of the Arthurian legend *Arthur, High King of Britain*, the magic of the epic story with its chivalry, romance, battles and betrayals is retained and the tales are told simply, in accessible language. In an example of how legends can be used in the crafting of new fiction, Philip Reeve demonstrates in *Here Lies Arthur* how the legends about Arthur could have emanated from rumours perpetrated by the spin doctor Merlin. When Gwyna becomes servant to the bard Myrrdin, she sees how trickery and storytelling – not magic and valour – are used to transform Arthur from just another brutal war-band leader to hero and future King of Britain. Gwyna herself changes from girl to the Lady of the Lake to boy while caught up in Myrrdin's plan to make Arthur a legend and so unite the country.

How the Whale Became and Other Tales of the Early World collects together all Ted Hughes' glorious inventions about how the earth's creatures came to be. The God in these stories is no all-seeing, all-knowing being, but an inventor and craftsman toiling joyously in his work-shop, fashioning all manner of animals and birds to unleash into the world. The mythic quality and respect for nature raw in tooth and claw which are so evident in Hughes' poetry are also present here, albeit often tempered with humour.

In *Monster Slayer* poet Brian Patten retells the legend of Beowulf for a young audience. The monster Grendel appears from 'the fens and foul-smelling marshland beyond the forest' and proceeds to demolish the King's Great Hall and tear apart his sleeping warriors. Enter, some years later, the young man Beowulf as the time to face Grendel 'is written in the stars'. The story of how he dispenses with the monster and his mother is told in modern language which still evokes the essence of an older time in the use of dialogue and verse. Chris Riddell's illustrations are vignettes which illuminate yet leave room for the imagination.

Traditional tales of all kinds are often played with for the enjoyment of readers and listeners who are familiar with the stories, for example disrupting conventional story structures and springing surprises. Examples include *Hungry Hen* by Richard Waring and Caroline Jayne Church, Lauren Child's *Beware of the Storybook Wolves* and *Who's Afraid of the Big Bad Book?*, several titles by Jon Scieszka, including *The Stinky Cheeseman and Other Fairly Stupid Tales*, and *The Sleeper and the Spindle* by Neil Gaiman and Chris Riddell.

CLASSIC FICTION

Books that have become classics of children's literature are also often given many interpretations, stories so familiar even when the original has not been read that they have become part of society's mental furniture.

In British children's literature, these include Frances Hodgson Burnett's *The Secret Garden* and Kenneth Grahame's *The Wind in the Willows*, but there are many more that today's teachers will know from their own childhoods and which still endure and are important to include in classroom collections in the 21st century. One of the most iconic is Lewis Carroll's *Alice's Adventures in Wonderland* and its sequel *Through the Looking Glass*. Artists around the world have been inspired to create new illustrations. The characters, the episodes and the images, particularly from John Tenniel's illustrations, have permeated culture in a variety of media including film and advertising and stimulated many writers – two recent examples being *Wonderland: Alice in Poetry* edited by Michaela Morgan, and a collection of short stories inspired by Alice *Return to Wonderland*.

Many well-known stories were first written in languages other than English. This certainly applies to traditional stories but also to classics such as Tove Jansson's *Moomin* stories and Erich Kästner's *Emil and the Detectives*. A small proportion of contemporary children's books are translated into English. However, enthusiasm has developed in recent years to seek out and promote children's literature in translation and offer English-speaking children access to a wider range of voices and ideas.

GENRE FICTION

There isn't space here to discuss all fictional genres but here are some examples of a few.

DETECTIVE AND MYSTERY STORIES

Emil and the Detectives is often cited as important in the development of detective and mystery stories for children. Emil is robbed on the train on his way to Berlin to visit his grandmother. He joins up with a gang of children and they work together to apprehend the thief. First published in the 1930s, this book in which quick-witted children foil the grown-ups has influenced many detective stories since. Crime and detective fiction is extremely popular with adults and recent years have seen the rapid development of such stories for children, in particular featuring girl detectives. As well as providing exciting plot-driven adventures that develop into series encouraging further reading, well-written examples can also feature characters who grow and change and who children become attached to. Younger readers can enjoy the childhood cases solved by Clara Vulliamy's Dotty Detective and Kate Pankhurst's Mariella Mystery series. Older children can follow the adventures of Lauren St John's Laura Marlin and Kat Wolfe, Tanya Landman's Poppy Fields and Lauren Child's Ruby Redfort who first appeared as the favourite fiction of Clarice Bean, a prior invention of Lauren Child's. A multicultural, multi-faceted urban setting, convincingly drawn central characters and fast-moving plots with plenty of comic moments are at the heart of Elen Caldecott's Marsh Road series. *High-Rise Mystery* by Sharna Jackson features a black detective duo, Nik and Norva.

Many detective series have historical settings, including the successful *Sinclair's Mysteries* by Katherine Woodfine set in an Edwardian department store, whose two central characters branch out in a subsequent series becoming international spies, and Robin Stevens' *Murder Most Unladylike Mysteries* series set in a 1930s boarding school, with all the trapping of girls' school stories of the period from midnight feasts to the relationships engendered by living in such a closely knit community, cleverly combining two popular genres.

HISTORICAL FICTION

Teachers will often seek historical fiction with cross-curricular links. However, finding good fiction accessible to the relevant age group can be problematic. It is almost always better to find a really engaging text that has the potential for links with other areas of the curriculum rather than vice versa. Historical fiction can be explored and enjoyed for other reasons than finding out information about past times and often aids empathetic understanding as well as having exciting and interesting plots. Well-known examples include Michelle Magorian's *Goodnight, Mister Tom* about a World War 2 evacuee and his relationship with the elderly man he is lodged with, and Berlie Doherty's *Street Child* in which the reader gains insight into living and working conditions for poor children in the 1860s while travelling alongside orphan Jim Jarvis. In John Boyne's *Stay Where You Are and Then Leave*, Alfie is five when World War 1 breaks out and his milkman father enlists in the army. Although this is a third-person narrative the story is seen very much through his eyes. As the war goes on, Alfie takes responsibility, secretly supplementing the family income and carrying out a mission to find out what has happened to his father. The situations faced by conscientious objectors, shell-shocked soldiers and neighbours who are interned are woven into the story which is immersed in everyday detail, giving the reading experience an almost tangible feel.

Jacqueline Wilson is best known for her contemporary stories featuring a range of modern families. Several of her more recent books have settings in the past including the *Hetty Feather* series set in Victorian times, *Queenie* which takes places in 1953, and *Opal Plumstead* in which the title character gets involved in the women's suffrage movement. Catherine Johnson's *Freedom* is a powerful story of Nathaniel, a slave brought from Jamaica to England in the 18th century, which manages to marry authentically told and harrowing history with humour, compassion and hope. In Henrietta Branford's *Fire, Bed and Bone* life at the time of the Peasants' Revolt is chronicled from the viewpoint of a dog. This device is amazingly powerful and the dog is able to make pertinent comments revealing much about the society of the time in language that conveys the atmosphere of the period.

ANIMAL FICTION

Novels that are convincingly narrated by animal characters are relatively rare but animals abound in children's literature. They may be humans in disguise or featured in their natural state. Either way, the picture books that feature bears, mice and rabbits are countless. For example, Martin Waddell and Barbara Firth's soothing *Can't You Sleep, Little Bear?* is really about a loving parent and child relationship. There are some excellent stories about relation-ships between people and animals that also comment on the human condition. In Sara Pennypacker's *Pax*, Peter and his tame fox are parted when his father goes away to war. Boy and fox each embark on an emotional and physical journey. Will reunion be possible? Sara Pennypacker manages to convey what may be in the mind of the fox without anthropomor-phising the animal. The language used evokes all the senses and both words and pictures are beautifully subtle in this moving novel. Animals and birds play important roles in most of Gill Lewis's novels but they are never anthropomorphised. In *Sky Hawk* two children res-cue an osprey in the Scottish Highlands. When tragedy strikes, one of them carries out a promise to protect the bird and tracks its migratory flight to the mangrove forests of the Gambia via the internet with some heartstopping moments along the way. A moving story involving the inspirational interconnection between humans and respect for wildlife.

ILLUSTRATED FICTION

In our visual age illustration has increasingly become important in children's narrative fiction not only in picture books. Pictures may not only be complementary to the text – they may also extend it. Examples in books for younger children are Philip Reeve and Sarah McIntyre's books which include *Oliver and the Seawigs* and *Pugs of the Frozen North*, Alex T. Smith's *Claude* series, Julian Gough and Jim Field's *Rabbit & Bear* series. Illustration in fiction for older children has a significant place too, for example Jim Kay's pictures in *A Monster Calls* written by Patrick Ness, David Roberts' for *Tinder* by Sally Gardner, and David Litchfield's for *War is Over* by David Almond.

Illustration is a vital part of some of the books that appeal to many children's taste, such as Jeff Kinney's *Diary of a Wimpy Kid* and Liz Pichon's *Tom Gates* series, and is a significant element of their recognition as a brand that children buy in to. Recognition in this way also plays a part in the importance of Nick Sharratt's illustrations in Jacqueline Wilson's fiction. However, here they also lighten the mood to some of the dark subjects she tackles.

"A RICH READING DIET WILL INCLUDE A RANGE OF TEXTS, SOME OF WHICH WILL BE ENJOYED BUT QUICKLY FORGOTTEN, AND IT IS REALLY IMPORTANT TO LISTEN TO AND RESPECT CHILDREN'S CHOICES WHILST HELPING THEM TO BROADEN THEIR READING RANGE. CHILDREN CAN EASILY BE PUT OFF WHEN THEY FEEL ADULTS ARE MAKING JUDGEMENTS ABOUT THEIR READING CHOICES."

A rich reading diet will include a range of texts, some of which will be enjoyed but quickly forgotten, and it is really important to listen to and respect children's choices whilst helping them to broaden their reading range. Children can easily be put off when they feel adults are making judgements about their reading choices, so to help them move forward in their reading, teachers have found it helpful to allow children to have a say in the selection of books for the book corner and library. By ensuring they have a wide knowledge of children's literature themselves – or by knowing where to look for informed recommendations – teachers have found they can encourage children to try new books, deepen their responses, and make connections by exploring other texts by the same author or on the same theme. A small detail or a real-life experience may make a significant link in an individual's mind.

It has only been possible to mention a small number of the amazing range of fiction for children available in today's world. A list of resources which are frequently updated is appended to this chapter to help teachers expand and update their knowledge and find the right book for the right child at the right time.

REFERENCES

Andersen, H.C. (2004) *Fairy Tales*, translated by Tiina Nunnally. London: Penguin.

Chiaet, J. (2013) Novel reading: Reading literary fiction improves empathy. *Scientific American*. www.scientificamerican.com/article/novel-finding-reading-literary-fiction-improves-empathy/ accessed 25/9/19.

Court, J. and Hahn, D. (2017) *A World of Books in Translation*. Swindon: School Library Association.

Cunningham, A. and Stanovich, K. (1998) What reading does for the mind. *American Educator*, 22.

Gaiman, N. (2013) Reading Agency lecture 2013: Reading and obligation given at the Barbican Centre, London, 14 October. https://readingagency.org.uk/news/blog/neil-gaiman-lecture-in-full.html accessed 25/9/19.

Hammond, C. (2019) *Does Reading Fiction Make Us Better People?* http://www.bbc.com/future/story/20190523-does-reading-fiction-make-us-better-people accessed 25/9/19

Hardy, B. (1977) 'Towards a poetics of fiction: an approach through narrative', in M. Meek, A. Warlow and G. Barton (eds), *The Cool Web: The Pattern of Children's Reading*. London: Bodley Head.

Krashen, S.D. (2004) *The Power of Reading: Insights from the Research*. Portsmouth, NH/Westport, CN: Libraries Unlimited.

O'Sullivan, O. and McGonigle, S. (2010) Transforming readers: Teachers and children in the Centre for Literacy in Primary Education Power of Reading project, *Literacy (UKLA)*, 44(2): 51-9.

Perrault, C. (2010) *The Complete Fairy Tales*, translated by Christopher Betts. Oxford: Oxford University Press.

Pullman, P. (2012) *Grimm Tales for Young and Old*. London: Penguin.

Rosenblatt, L. (1978) *The Reader, the Text, the Poem: The Transactional Theory of the Literary Work*. Carbondale: Southern Illinois University Press.

Smith, F. (2012) *Understanding Reading: A Psycholinguistic Analysis of Reading and Learning to Read*, 6th edition. Abingdon: Routledge.

RESOURCES

Armadillo Children's Book Review Magazine www.armadillomagazine.co.uk

Books for Keeps http://booksforkeeps.co.uk/

Booktrust www.booktrust.org.uk

Carousel magazine www.carouselguide.co.uk/

CLPE core booklist www.clpe.org.uk/corebooks

CLPE thematic and author booklists www.clpe.org.uk/library/booklists

Down the Rabbit Hole A monthly podcast about children's literature http://dtrhradio.com/

Love Reading for Kids www.lovereading4kids.co.uk

Reading Zone www.readingzone.com

The School Librarian The quarterly journal of the School Library Association www.sla.org.uk

FiND OUT MORE

Barrs, M. and Cork, V. (2001) *The Reader in the Writer*. London: Centre for Literacy in Primary Education.

Chambers, A. (2011) *Tell Me: Children, Reading and Talk with The Reading Environment*. Stroud: The Thimble Press.

CLPE (2018) *Choosing and Using Quality Children' Texts: What We Know Works*. London: Centre for Literacy in Primary Education. Downloadable from https://clpe.org.uk/library-and-resources/what-we-know-works-booklets

Gamble, N. (2019) *Exploring Children's Literature*, 4th edition. London: Sage.

Goodwin, P. (ed.) (2008) *Understanding Children's Books*. London: Sage.

Mallett, M. (2010) *Choosing and Using Fiction and Non-Fiction 3-11*. Abingdon: Routledge.

CHiLDREN'S BOOKS REFERENCED iN THiS CHAPTER

Almond, D. (2018) *War is Over*, illustrated by David Litchfield. London: Hodder.

Anderson, S. (2018) *The House with Chicken Legs*, illustrated by Elisa Paganelli. London: Usborne.

Boyne, J. (2013) *Stay Where You Are and Then Leave*. London: Doubleday.

Branford, H. (1997, 2018) *Fire, Bed and Bone*. London: Walker.

Bunzl, P. et al. (2019) *Return to Wonderland: Stories Inspired by Lewis Carroll's Alice*, illustrated by Laura Barrett. London: Macmillan.

Burnett, F.H. (1911) *The Secret Garden*. Current editions available include those published by Walker (2013) with illustrations by Inga Moore and Puffin Classics (2008).

Caldecott, E. (2015) *Diamonds and Daggers*. London: Bloomsbury. First in the Marsh Road Mysteries series.

Carroll, L. (1865) *Alice's Adventures in Wonderland*, illustrated by John Tenniel. London: Macmillan.

Carroll, L. (1871) *Through the Looking Glass*, illustrated by John Tenniel. London: Macmillan.

Child, L. (2000, 2012) *Beware of the Storybook Wolves*. London: Hodder, Orchard.

Child, L. (2002, 2012) *Who's Afraid of the Big Bad Book?* London: Hodder; Orchard.

Child, L. (2012) *Look into My Eyes*. London: HarperCollins. First in the Ruby Redfort series.

Child, L. (2003) *Clarice Bean, Utterly Me*. London: Orchard.

Crossley-Holland, K. (2018) *Between Worlds: Folktales of Britain & Ireland*, illustrated by Frances Castle. London: Walker.

Doherty, B. (2000, 2016) *Fairy Tales*, illustrated by Jane Ray. London: Walker.

Doherty, B. (1993) *Street Child*. London: HarperCollins.

Duffy, C.A. (2014) *Faery Tales*, illustrated by Tomislav Tomic. London: Faber & Faber.

Gaiman, N. (2014) *The Sleeper and the Spindle*, illustrated by Chris Riddell. London: Bloomsbury.

Gardner, S. (2013) *Tinder*, illustrated by David Roberts. London: Orion.

Gavin, J. (2013) *Blackberry Blue*, illustrated by Richard Collingridge. London: Tamarind.

Gough, J. and Field, J. (2016) *Rabbit & Bear: Rabbit's Bad Habits*. London: Hodder. First in the Rabbit & Bear series.

Hughes, T. (2018) *How the Whale Became and Other Tales of the Early World*. London: Faber & Faber. [First published in 2003 under the title *The Dreamfighter and Other Creation Tales*.]

Jackson, S. (2019) *High-Rise Mystery*. London: Knights Of.

Jaffrey, M. (1985; 1992) *Seasons of Splendour: Tales, Myths & Legends of India*, illustrated by Michael Foreman. London: Pavilion in association with Michael Joseph, Puffin.

Jansson, T. (1945, 2012) *The Moomins and the Great Flood*. London: Sort Of Books. The first of the Moomin stories. Most recent translation into English by David McDuff (2012).

Johnson, C. (2018) *Freedom*. London: Scholastic.

Jones, D.W. (2000) *Eight Days of Luke*, illustrated by David Wyatt. London: HarperCollins [first published by Macmillan 1975].

Kästner, E. (1929) *Emil and the Detectives*. Current edition published by Red Fox Classics (2001), illustrated by Walter Trier, translated by Eileen Hall.

Kinney, J. (2008) *Diary of a Wimpy Kid*. London: Puffin. First in the Wimpy Kid series.

Landman, T. (2013) *Mondays Are Murder*. London: Walker. First in the Poppy Fields series.

Lewis, G. (2011) *Sky Hawk*. Oxford: Oxford University Press.

Lupton, H. and Morden, D. (2006) *The Adventures of Odysseus*, illustrated by Christina Balit. Bath: Barefoot Books.

Magorian, M. (1981, 1983) *Goodnight, Mister Tom*. London: Kestrel/Puffin.

Mhlophe, G. (2009) *African Tales*, illustrated by Rachel Griffin. Bath: Barefoot Books.

Morgan, M. (ed.) (2016) *Wonderland: Alice in Poetry*, illustrated by John Tenniel. London: Macmillan.

Morpurgo, M. (1994, 2010) *Arthur, High King of Britain*, illustrated by Michael Foreman. London: Pavilion/Egmont.

Ness, P. (2011) *A Monster Calls*, illustrated by Jim Kay. London: Walker.

Pankhurst, K. (2013) *The Ghostly Guinea Pig*. London: Orion. First in the Mariella Mystery series.

Patten, B. (2016) *Monster Slayer*, illustrated by Chris Riddell. Edinburgh: Barrington Stoke.

Pennypacker, S. (2016) *Pax*, illustrated by Jon Klassen. London: HarperCollins.

Pichon, L. (2011) *The Brilliant World of Tom Gates*. London: Scholastic. First in the Tom Gates series.

Reeve, P. (2007) *Here Lies Arthur*. London: Scholastic.

Reeve, P. and McIntyre, S. (2013) *Oliver and the Seawigs*. Oxford: Oxford University Press.

Reeve, P. and McIntyre, S. (2015) *Pugs of the Frozen North*. Oxford: Oxford University Press.

St John, L. (2011) *Dead Man's Cove*, illustrated by David Dean. London: Orion. First in the Laura Marlin Mystery series.

St John, L. (2018) *Kat Wolfe Investigates*, illustrated by Beidi Guo. London: Macmillan. First in the Wolfe and Lamb Mysteries series.

Scieszka, J. (1993) *The Stinky Cheeseman and Other Fairly Stupid Tales*, illustrated by Lane Smith. London: Puffin.

Scieszka, J. (1991) *The True Story of the 3 Little Pigs by A. Wolf*, illustrated by Lane Smith. London: Puffin.

Scieszka, J. (1994) *The Frog Prince Continued*, illustrated by Steve Johnson. London: Puffin.

Smith, A.T. (2011) *Claude in the City*. London: Hodder. First in the Claude series.

Stevens, R. (2014) *Murder Most Unladylike*. London: Puffin. First in the Murder Most Unladylike series.

Vulliamy, C. (2016) *Dotty Detective*. London: HarperCollins. First in the Dotty Detective series.

Waddell, M. (1988) *Can't You Sleep, Little Bear?* illustrated by Barbara Firth. London: Walker.

Waring, R. (2001) *Hungry Hen*, illustrated by Caroline Jayne Church. Oxford: Oxford University Press.

Williams, M. (1991, 2006) *Greek Myths*. London: Walker.

Williams, M. (1996) *The Iliad and the Odyssey*. London: Walker.

Wilson, J. (2009) *Hetty Feather*, illustrated by Nick Sharratt. London: Doubleday. First in the Hetty Feather series.

Wilson, J. (2014) *Opal Plumstead*, illustrated by Nick Sharratt. London: Doubleday.

Wilson, J. (2013) *Queenie*, illustrated by Nick Sharratt. London: Doubleday.

Woodfine, K. (2015) *The Mystery of the Clockwork Sparrow*. London: Egmont. First in the Sinclair's Mysteries series.

CHAPTER 4

NON-FICTION TEXTS IN THE PRIMARY SCHOOL

ANN LAZIM

This chapter explores non-fiction as an equal partner with fiction in the primary school, performing different although sometimes overlapping functions. Non-fiction can be closely related to curriculum topics and also enjoyed as an important element of reading for pleasure, although these two aspects need not be mutually exclusive. Some key features of good information texts are described and recent trends in information book publishing are highlighted.

THE IMPORTANCE OF NON-FICTION

Access to good non-fiction is important as part of a broader curriculum. It is also significant in children's wider reading diet. Discussions about reading for pleasure too often focus exclusively on fiction, but high quality information books that present facts in an interesting and informative way are a key part of any classroom collection. Non-fiction books are often excellent examples of how text and pictures can work together to provide comprehensive information and an enjoyable reading experience.

"NON-FICTION CAN OFTEN BE A USEFUL WAY OF ENGAGING READERS WHO SHOW LITTLE INTEREST IN READING FICTION."

Non-fiction can often be a useful way of engaging readers who show little interest in reading fiction. Well-presented factual subject matter, usually combined with illustration, can be inviting for more reluctant readers. As with fiction, children's own tastes and interests should be taken into account when building a non-fiction collection for a classroom. Too often the temptation is to limit information books to curriculum subjects, but just as with fiction a balance of subject matter, styles, authors and illustrators need to be considered as you put together a classroom collection.

Reading non-fiction is important in terms of developing critical reading, i.e.evaluating accuracy and the validity of sources – a crucial skill in our modern world which extends to looking at other sources of information, particularly those online. For a time it looked as though the publishing of non-fiction books for children was in decline as people turned to the internet for information. However, there has been a renaissance in information book publishing with much more attention being paid to illustration and design, as well as an increasing recognition of the interconnectedness of knowledge rather than as isolated topics. Just as in the adult market, publishers realise that children have a range of preferences and have created a variety of different kinds of texts. It is important that children see that variety in their classrooms as much as possible.

THE KEY FEATURES OF A GOOD INFORMATION TEXT

It could generally be said that the features of a good information book would include a contents list, an index, good illustrations and/or photographs, labels, captions, clear headings, and where appropriate a glossary, diagrams and maps. However, this cannot be universally applied, for example where much narrative non-fiction is concerned. Other matters to consider include the expertise of the author and their approach to the subject for a child audience, and the design of the book and its likely appeal to young people.

Imaginative and varied use of language is not only the province of fiction. For example, Owen Davey's animal books with their alliterative titles *Mad about Monkeys, Smart about Sharks, Crazy about Cats, Bonkers about Beetles, Fanatical about Frogs*, combine a chatty, informal and interactive style with specialised vocabulary. '*"But why such colourful bums?"* I hear you ask' is combined with specialised vocabulary, i.e. 'Many species of Old World monkeys have strange sitting pads on their bottoms called **ischial callosities**' (Davey, 2015: 11).

THE EXPERTISE AND KNOWLEDGE OF THE AUTHOR

Authors of information texts need to have an understanding of and enthusiasm for their subject and the ability to convey this to children. It is ideal when the author is an expert in the subject but this is not always possible. Excellent non-fiction texts on subjects with high levels of interest for young readers have been produced by publishers such as Usborne whose information books are largely researched and written by their experienced in-house team.

Nicola Davies is the author of many information books for children, and she brings her expertise as a zoologist to many of them plus an understanding of children through direct engagement and her experience as a media presenter. She is equally at home writing verse and poetic prose and lively factual texts about subjects ranging from poo to parasites, bats to bears, sharks to snakes. She has been paired with many outstanding illustrators whose artwork complements her writing. In *Tiny: The Invisible World of Microbes*, illustrated by Emily Sutton, a combination of imaginative language and illustrations demonstrates the enormous role played in the world by microscopic life forms. Understanding is gradually built from a simple and enticing opening by means of evocative comparisons, such as equating the number of microbes in a teaspoon of soil with the population of India. Readers discover what microbes are, what they do, and how fast they multiply. There is a wealth of fascinating facts but the presentation ensures this is not overwhelming. *White Owl, Barn Owl* is another of Davies' books and an example of the way in which narrative and non-fiction can work together. Illustrated by Michael Foreman and published in Walker Books' Nature Storybooks series, a child and her grandfather watch a family of barn owls nesting in a box that they have placed in a tree to help protect them from predators, as the trees and barns where they usually make their homes have been destroyed. Their close relationship is evident in the way the grandfather gives explanations at the same time as encouraging the child to make her own observations. The central narrative is from the child's viewpoint. Additional facts about barn owls appear on each spread in a different font. The main text and some vignettes appear on a sepia background while Michael Foreman's signature palette of shades of blue is perfect for the night-time scenes portrayed in the larger illustrations. A basic index is included so that children can get used to this means of accessing information within a text from an early age.

Children's literature is especially rich in information books about the natural world and animals in particular. There are also numerous books about history. The author/illustrator team of Mick Manning and Brita Granström has produced information books on a variety of subjects for a wide age range with enthusiasm and insight, excelling in the area of telling stories about history with reference to individuals in their context. Some of their books focus on the experiences of Mick Manning's own family and they always draw on the expertise of authorities in relevant organisations, especially museums. In *Charlie's War Illustrated: Remembering World War One* and *My Uncle's Dunkirk*, both published in association with the Imperial War Museum, Mick Manning draws on the experiences of members of his own family to give personalised descriptions of the two world wars. Pictures of contemporary photographs, cards and telegrams are integrated with Brita Granström's illustrations. *Charlie's War Illustrated* is related from the viewpoint of Mick's grandfather. The poignant story of his uncle's experiences during World War II has been pieced together from souvenirs discovered after he died because, as Mick reiterates throughout the book, 'he never spoke about it'.

In their *William Shakespeare: Scenes from the Life of the World's Greatest Writer*, produced in association with the Shakespeare Birthplace Trust, readers are taken through Shakespeare's life from his childhood in Stratford-upon-Avon to his final years there, with his time on the London stage in between. His story is contextualised with information about the historical period, particularly contemporary theatre. The text is in the present tense which lends immediacy and there are apposite quotes from his plays at the opening of each section. Summaries of the plots of many of his plays are set out in an accessible comic strip format.

HISTORY AND BIOGRAPHY – WHOSE VOICES?

Seeking out the work of authors who are writing from authentic personal experience and knowledge is as important with non-fiction as it is with fiction.

"SEEKING OUT THE WORK OF AUTHORS WHO ARE WRITING FROM AUTHENTIC PERSONAL EXPERIENCE AND KNOWLEDGE IS AS IMPORTANT WITH NON-FICTION AS IT IS WITH FICTION. THE QUESTION OF VIEWPOINT IS ESPECIALLY SIGNIFICANT."

The question of viewpoint is especially significant in history and young people need to be taught to consider critically whose stories are being told. As Margaret Meek says in *Information and Book Learning* (Meek, 1996: 54), 'when do young learners discover that there is more than one way to interpret the past?' and 'What alerts the young to the silences of historians?'. She was asking these questions more than twenty years ago and they are still important to ask, particularly when thinking about the representation of global diversity and perspective in classroom collections.

The success of *Good Night Stories for Rebel Girls* by Elena Favilli and Francesca Cavallo, and Kate Pankhurst's *Fantastically Great Women Who Changed the World* and their sequels, has inspired a whole range of books containing brief biographies of pioneering women across a range of spheres, times and places. Some take a similar general approach while others focus on a specific area of achievement, such as Rachel Ignotofsky's *Women in Science* and *Women in Sport*, and *The Bigger Picture: Women Who Changed the Art World* by Sophia Bennett and Manjit Thapp. Vashti Harrison has highlighted the lives of black women in *Little Leaders: Bold Women in Black History*, and a wider range of ethnically diverse women in *Little Leaders: Visionary Women Around the World*, while Siobhán Parkinson has described Irish women's contributions in *Rocking the System: Fearless and Amazing Irish Women Who Made History*. These biographical compilations have become quite a phenomenon and are one way in which the stories of underrepresented people are being made available to children. The focus on women detailed above has now extended to books that highlight the lives of men who have led less conventional lives, such as *Stories for Boys Who Dare to be Different* by Ben Brooks and *The Good Guys: 50 Heroes Who Changed the World with Kindness* by Rob Kemp. *Young, Gifted and Black: Meet 52 Black Heroes from Past and Present*, by Jamia Wilson and Andrea Pippins, has brief biographical sketches of black achievers from around the world, with a particular focus on African Americans.

The publication of individual biographies is an expanding area, with the distinctive *Little People, Big Dreams* series originated by Maria Isabel Sánchez Vegara for younger children leading the way in increasing the range and diversity of people written about for young people. In general, individual biographies for children have previously focused on a fairly narrow range of people, partly down to publishers' perception of what will sell in schools. A shifting of the market towards parents and carers increasingly buying books that are for entertainment as well as being obviously educational, in addition to schools recognising the importance of reading for pleasure, may be influencing the wider range that is becoming available.

NARRATIVE NON-FICTION AND THE CROSSOVER WITH FICTION

It is perhaps no surprise that information texts that employ narrative have increased as there is greater recognition that the human mind is inclined to find story an aid to understanding (Hardy, 1977). Biographies and autobiographies are clearly a part of this if they tell life stories in a linear fashion. Some biographies for adults now take a thematic approach but this is rare in books for children.

One aspect of this is a crossover between fiction and non-fiction. An example is the *Voices* series edited by the author Tony Bradman and described by the publisher as a 'narrative non-fiction series about the unsung voices of our past'. The first title, *Now or Never: A Dunkirk Story* by Bali Rai, gives a perspective on the evacuation of Dunkirk by a young Muslim soldier, and *Diver's Daughter: A Tudor Story* by Patrice Lawrence, is related from the viewpoint of a black girl in Elizabethan England. Whilst the central characters and their stories are fictional, the historical details have been well researched and the novels inspired by the authors' own questioning about the past.

There are, therefore, many different kinds of non-fiction texts and an important consideration for teachers choosing their book stock is to make sure that there is a balance of style and perspective – even about the same subject. Sometimes fiction can give readers greater empathy and knowledge than an information book with a conventional layout. For example, there are several books about dinosaur discoverer and fossil hunter Mary Anning, such as *History VIPs: Mary Anning* by Kay Barnham, that set out the chronological details of her life and her contribution to palaeontology, and place these in their social and historical context, using the format of double-page spreads with framed gobbets of related information. However, fiction can often give great insights and be more than just an interesting adjunct to a more conventional information book. Two picture books relate elements of Mary Anning's life. *Stone Girl Bone Girl* by Laurence Anholt and Sheila Moxley focuses on dramatic incidents, enticing readers to find out more. Spiritual, almost supernatural elements are introduced into the story, e.g. Mary was struck by lightning as a baby, and also the little dog who helps her to find the ichthyosaurus embedded in the cliff at Lyme Regis mysteriously disappears afterwards. The influence of her father on her developing interest in fossils is emphasised. *The Fossil Girl* by Catherine Brighton focuses more specifically on the episode in which she finds the ichthyosaur. The text is briefer and the comic strip-style illustrations convey the light and colour of a seaside town. Mary is portrayed as a more independent character in this version. A novel, *Lightning Mary* by Anthea Simmons, in which Mary's story is told from her point of view, really gives a feel for the historical period without using archaic language. The author's research is woven seamlessly into the story and it always feels as though the details are germane to the telling. There is an afterword in which the author writes about the factual basis for the novel, notes about fossils and fossil-hunting, and interestingly, from an educational viewpoint, there is an endorsement from an organisation that aims to inspire and support girls and women into STEM industries. *Lightning Mary* touches on 19th century attitudes towards the tensions between religion and scientific discovery and women's roles linked to this, as does Frances Hardinge's award-winning *The Lie Tree*.

APPROACHES TO SCIENCE

History is not the only subject where facts are incorporated into fiction. Christopher Edge's novels *The Many Worlds of Albie Bright, The Infinite Lives of Maisie Day, The Jamie Drake Equation* and *The Longest Night of Charlie Noon* all draw on scientific facts, concepts and ideas, and the books refer to other links on a website.

There are also inventive approaches to science in a picture-book format. The *Professor Astro Cat* books are written by physicist Dr Dominic Walliman. They capture the excitement of finding out about science although children who already know a lot will find new facts to intrigue them. Beautifully designed combinations of up-to-date text written by an expert in the field are integrated within illustrations by artist Ben Newman whose use of shape and colour renders a retro feel. The use of Professor Astro Cat as a guide is an appealing device. His voice is humorous and authoritative, presenting complex ideas in an accessible way. *Professor Astro Cat's Frontiers of Space* was followed by *Professor Astro Cat's Atomic Adventure* and *Professor Astro Cat's Human Body Odyssey*, and the need for a simplified version of some the information in the first book for a younger audience has been answered by *Professor Astro Cat's Solar System*, where the information is deliberately limited to facts contained in three speech bubbles per spread so as not to overwhelm younger readers with information. Access to these books needs to be via dipping in and reading the clear headings for each page as there are no indexes although they have glossaries. Another engaging approach to scientific subjects can be found in James Carter's poetry picture books including *Once Upon a Star: A Poetic Journey Through Space*, illustrated by Mar Hernández. Other titles are *Once Upon a Raindrop: The Story of Water*, illustrated by Nomoco, *The Big Beyond. The Story of Space Travel*, illustrated by Aaron Cushley, and *Once Upon a Rhythm: The Story of Music*, illustrated by Valerio Vidali.

DESIGN AND FORMAT

Recent trends in information book design, partly in response to the advent of the internet as a source of information, include a move away from photographs to illustration. In particular, the success of the large-format *Maps* by Aleksandra Mizielińska and Daniel Mizieliński has resulted in the production of interesting atlases that illustrate geographical themes in a host of ways. This particular design innovation is new but illustration-led information books are not. In 1996 Margaret Meek commented, 'Nowadays designers of books for learning pay as much attention, sometimes more, to what readers look at as to what they read' (Meek, 1996: 44).

She also commented that this design-led approach has resulted in the production of information books by teams of people rather than being 'the composition of a single author or artist' (Meek, 1996: 44). She cites the work of publisher Dorling Kindersley whose photographic approach was groundbreaking and much imitated.

It is important to recognise that texts need not always be books. This is the case across the full range of literature but perhaps has particular pertinence when it comes to information texts. While the focus here is on books, children need to explore a variety of formats and approaches including multi-media and internet information sources.

WAYS IN WHICH SCHOOLS HAVE USED INFORMATION TEXTS IN THEIR CURRICULUM TO INSPIRE READING FOR PLEASURE

In *Yucky Worms* by Vivian French and Jessica Ahlberg, a boy learns from observing worms in the garden alongside his grandmother that they are not so yucky after all. He finds out that their eating and excretion habits are helpful in recycling material which is good for the soil and helps plants grow. Gran dispels the myth that cutting worms in half doesn't hurt them. The informative ongoing intergenerational conversation is supplemented by facts integrated with illustrations which are more diagrammatic than the central pictures.

This has been a very popular book with EYFS children and their teachers, enabling cross-curricular links, outdoor play, and with an appeal for boys and girls. One teacher described how the work around this book had gone on for weeks. The class had a wormery and children were taking home worms in their pockets. There was more feedback from parents than ever before – commenting that they were learning too. One 4-year-old girl got her parents to lie on the floor and stamped so they could understand what it was like to be a blind worm with the only the sound and feeling of vibrations to warn you that you were prey for a bird. The teacher of another EYFS class reported on the enjoyment centred around this book with the class creating a worm journal and a worm farm.

Shackleton's Journey by William Grill won the 2015 CILIP Kate Greenaway Medal for illustration, a rare event for an information book. In this large-format book William Grill weaves a detailed visual narrative of Shackleton's journey to Antarctica. His beautiful use of coloured pencils and vibrant hues effortlessly evokes the adventure and excitement that surrounded the expedition. His impeccably researched drawings, rich with detail, fastidiously reproduce the minutiae of the expedition. Children love examining the diagrams of the peculiar provisions and the individual drawings of each sled dog and packhorse. This book takes the academic and historical information behind the expedition and reinterprets it for a young audience.

A teacher of a Year 6 reported that the children had not really experienced a book like *Shackleton's Journey* before and they loved it. They found the facts interesting, especially the research about the crew. They had limited knowledge about exploration before this. At the time they were working with the book there was some news about an explorer going to the South Pole which tied in and enabled them to make links with the real world.

A teacher of another Upper KS2 class found that the children related to the book much more than he expected in view of the social class/cultural divide and the activity of writing CVs for people applying to go on the voyage, as he observed that the actual people who were accepted were mostly upper class.

CONCLUSION

It is important to recognise that children can get much pleasure from exploring information books for their own sake as well as using them to support the curriculum.

"IT IS IMPORTANT TO RECOGNISE THAT CHILDREN CAN GET MUCH PLEASURE FROM EXPLORING INFORMATION BOOKS FOR THEIR OWN SAKE AS WELL AS USING THEM TO SUPPORT THE CURRICULUM."

These texts may link with children's existing interests in ways that confirm and expand what they already know. They may also widen their horizons, sometimes in unexpected ways. Keeping the non-fiction book collections in your classroom book corner and school library up to date is vital, as the information in them can rapidly go out of date. Recent trends in the design and production of information books have led to them becoming more attractive to handle, including large-format books which children can share, exploring the words and pictures together.

REFERENCES

Davey, O. (2015) *Mad About Monkeys*. London: Flying Eye.
Christopher Edge website www.christopheredge.co.uk/
Hardy, B. (1977) 'Towards a poetics of fiction: an approach through narrative', in M. Meek, A. Warlow and G. Barton (eds), *The Cool Web: The Pattern of Children's Reading*. London: Bodley Head.
Meek, M. (1996) *Information & Book Learning*. Stroud: The Thimble Press.

RESOURCES

Armadillo Children's Book Review Magazine www.armadillomagazine.co.uk
Books for Keeps http://booksforkeeps.co.uk/
Booktrust www.booktrust.org.uk
Carousel magazine www.carouselguide.co.uk/
CLPE core booklist www.clpe.org.uk/corebooks
CLPE thematic and author booklists www.clpe.org.uk/library/booklists
Down the Rabbit Hole A monthly podcast about children's literature http://dtrhradio.com/
Love Reading for Kids www.lovereading4kids.co.uk
Reading Zone www.readingzone.com
The School Librarian The quarterly journal of the School Library Association www.sla.org.uk

FIND OUT MORE

CLPE (2018) *Choosing and Using Quality Children' Texts: What We Know Works*. London: Centre for Literacy in Primary Education. https://clpe.org.uk/library-and-resources/what-we-know-works-booklets
Mallett, M. (2010) *Choosing and Using Fiction and Non-Fiction 3-11*. Abingdon: Routledge.

Mallett, M. (2003) *Early Years Non-Fiction*. Abingdon: Routledge.

Meek, M. (1996) *Information & Book Learning*. Stroud: The Thimble Press.

CHILDREN'S BOOKS REFERENCED IN THIS CHAPTER

Anholt, L. and Moxley, S. (2006) *Stone Girl Bone Girl: A Story of Mary Anning of Lyme Regis*. London: Frances Lincoln. [First published London: Doubleday 1999.]

Barnham, K. (2016) *History VIPs: Mary Anning*. London: Wayland.

Bennett, S. and Thapp, M. (2019) *The Bigger Picture: Women Who Changed the Art World*. London: Tate Publishing.

Brighton, C. (1999) *The Fossil Girl: Mary Anning's Dinosaur Discovery*. London: Lincoln Children's Books.

Brooks, B. (2018) *Stories for Boys Who Dare to be Different*, illustrated by Quinton Winter. London: Quercus.

Carter, J. (2018) *Once Upon a Star: A Poetic Journey through Space*, illustrated by Mar Hernández. London: Caterpillar Books.

Carter, J. (2018) *Once Upon a Raindrop: The Story of Water*, illustrated by Nomoco. London: Caterpillar Books.

Carter, J. (2019) *The Big Beyond: The Story of Space Travel*, illustrated by Aaron Cushley. London: Caterpillar Books.

Carter, J. (2019) *Once Upon a Rhythm: The Story of Music*, illustrated by Valerio Vidali. London: Caterpillar Books.

Davey, O. (2015) *Mad about Monkeys*. London: Flying Eye.

Davey, O. (2016) *Smart about Sharks*. London: Flying Eye.

Davey, O. (2017) *Crazy about Cats*. London: Flying Eye.

Davey, O. (2018) *Bonkers about Beetles*. London: Flying Eye.

Davey, O. (2019) *Fanatical about Frogs*. London: Flying Eye.

Davies, N. (2014) *Tiny: The Invisible World of Microbes*, illustrated by Emily Sutton. London: Walker.

Davies, N. (2007) *White Owl, Barn Owl*, illustrated by Michael Foreman. London: Walker.

Edge, C. (2016) *The Many Worlds of Albie Bright*, illustrated by Matt Saunders. London: Nosy Crow.

Edge, C. (2018) *The Infinite Lives of Maisie Day*, illustrated by Matt Saunders. London: Nosy Crow.

Edge, C. (2017) *The Jamie Drake Equation*, illustrated by Matt Saunders. London: Nosy Crow.

Edge, C. (2019) *The Longest Night of Charlie Noon*, illustrated by Matt Saunders. London: Nosy Crow.

Favilli, E. and Cavallo, F. (2017) *Good Night Stories for Rebel Girls*. London: Particular Books.

French, V. (2009) *Yucky Worms*, illustrated by Jessica Ahlberg. London: Walker.

Grill, W. (2014) *Shackleton's Journey*. London: Flying Eye.

Hardinge, F. (2015) *The Lie Tree*. London: Macmillan.

Harrison, V. (2018) *Little Leaders: Bold Women in Black History*. London: Puffin.

Harrison, V. (2018) *Little Leaders: Visionary Women Around the World*. London: Puffin

Ignotofsky, R. (2017) *Women in Science: 50 Fearless Pioneers Who Changed the World*. London: Wren & Rook.

Ignotofsky, R. (2018) *Women in Sport: 50 Fearless Athletes Who Played to Win*. London: Wren & Rook.

Kemp, R. (2018) *The Good Guys: 50 Heroes Who Changed the World with Kindness*. London: Wren & Rook.

Lawrence, P. (2019) *Diver's Daughter: A Tudor Story*. London: Scholastic.

Manning, M. (2013) *Charlie's War Illustrated: Remembering World War One*, illustrated by Brita Granström. London: Watts.

Manning, M. (2010) *My Uncle's Dunkirk*, illustrated by Brita Granström. London: Watts.

Manning, M. (2015) *William Shakespeare: Scenes from the Life of the World's Greatest Writer*, illustrated by Brita Granström. London: Lincoln Children's Books.

Mizielińska, A. and Mizieliński, D. (2013) *Maps* (Big Picture Press).

Pankhurst, K. (2016) *Fantastically Great Women Who Changed the World*. London: Bloomsbury.

Parkinson, S. (2018) *Rocking the System: Fearless and Amazing Irish Women Who Made History*, illustrated by Bren Luke. Dublin: Little Island.

Rai, B. (2019) *Now or Never: A Dunkirk Story*. London: Scholastic.

Simmons, A. (2019) *Lightning Mary*. London: Andersen Press.

Sánchez Vegara, M.I. (2016 onwards) *Little People, Big Dreams* series. London: Lincoln Children's Books.

Walliman, D. (2013) *Professor Astro Cat's Frontiers of Space*, illustrated by Ben Newman. London: Flying Eye.

Walliman, D. (2016) *Professor Astro Cat's Atomic Adventure*, illustrated by Ben Newman. London: Flying Eye.

Walliman, D. (2018) *Professor Astro Cat's Human Body Odyssey*, illustrated by Ben Newman. London: Flying Eye.

Walliman, D. (2017) *Professor Astro Cat's Solar System*, illustrated by Ben Newman. London: Flying Eye.

Wilson, J. (2018) *Young, Gifted and Black: Meet 52 Black Heroes from Past and Present*, illustrated by Andrea Pippins. London: Wide-Eyed Editions.

CHAPTER 5

POETRY IN THE PRIMARY SCHOOL

CHARLOTTE HACKING

Poetry is one of the most important branches of literature, providing the gateway for so many young readers and writers in their journey towards becoming literate; delighting, supporting and engaging children as they build a love of literature. We are introduced to language and reading through the rhyme we hear and join in with as children and our poetry journey begins there. How well we travel along the road depends on how well exposed we are along the way to the joys and potential poetry offers to us as readers and writers. It is a central part of a successful rich reading classroom and a key aspect of learning to read and becoming a mature, independent reader.

So how do you become a good teacher of poetry? You read it, you respond to it, you even have a go at writing it. But to want to do this, you have to find the poetry that speaks to you, that excites you, that inspires you, and then you do the same for your children.

"SO HOW DO YOU BECOME A GOOD TEACHER OF POETRY? YOU READ IT, YOU RESPOND TO IT, YOU EVEN HAVE A GO AT WRITING IT. BUT TO WANT TO DO THIS, YOU HAVE TO FIND THE POETRY THAT SPEAKS TO YOU, THAT EXCITES YOU, THAT INSPIRES YOU, AND THEN YOU DO THE SAME FOR YOUR CHILDREN."

The wonderful thing about poetry is that it can be taught anywhere, at any time. Planned units around a particular collection or anthology will be a part of the curriculum at some point in the year, but throughout the year, regular opportunities for a range of essential experiences to develop children's knowledge of, engagement with and perceptions of poetry can be built in throughout the curriculum and school day.

OPPORTUNITIES TO HEAR POETRY READ ALOUD

The best way to engage children with poetry is to make sure they hear a wide range of poetry as often as possible. It is important to hear and feel the distinct rhythms of different voices, have time to consider what this adds to our own private interpretation, and for us to get a sense of how a poem makes us feel and what it makes us think about. Too many times, reading poetry leads straight to analysis, looking for interesting vocabulary, poetic devices or a deconstruction of the form, before children have had the chance to consider their likes and dislikes and the emotive responses a poem can evoke within them. As one of the teachers on CLPE's 2018 Power of Poetry project reflected:

> 'I have been, potentially, putting children off poetry by making its dissection so prominent. I was denying them the pure pleasure experienced by a poem dropped into the day – the chance to bask in words/thoughts without having to respond in any way at all. Even within a more structured process, where ultimately an outcome would be to consider the component parts, I was moving far too quickly into discussion of technique and devices. I no longer just teach children about the poetic forms and devices that poets use. I now work hard to absorb children in poetry and poets first.'

Listening to poetry regularly in class develops a shared culture and an understanding that poetry is important. Ensure poetry of all kinds is a prominent part of the reading environment. Take time to drop poems into the school day, without any agenda to analyse or answer questions about them. This could be at the start of the day, before break or lunchtime or at the end of a day. As children hear and read more poetry themselves, open up this experience so they can choose and share poems they have found. Share a range of poems that link to concepts in other curriculum areas as a stimulus for discussion and as part of displays of work and artefacts. Study poetic forms that link to particular themes and times, e.g. kennings in history when studying the Vikings.

If children are aware of a wide range and breadth of poetry and are introduced to new poets, voices and styles they may not meet through their own reading, they will begin to develop their own tastes and preferences. Teachers will often be surprised at the types of poetry children are interested in and respond to. When choosing poetry for children, try not to be judgemental about what you think they will like or dislike or what you think might be too difficult or narrow in choices about what constitutes poetry.

"CHILDREN DO NOT NEED TO IMMEDIATELY UNDERSTAND EVERY WORD OF A POEM BEFORE HEARING IT READ ALOUD. THEY WILL BEGIN TO GET A SENSE OF THE FEELING THE POEM EVOKES IN THEM AS IT IS READ."

Children do not need to immediately understand every word of a poem before hearing it read aloud. They will begin to get a sense of the feeling the poem evokes in them as it is read. Children can revel in the language and imagery of classic poetry, speculating on word meanings and themes as well as exploring a range of modern and new kinds of verse.

LISTENING TO POETS PERFORM THEIR WORK

Videos and audio performances of poets reading their poems aloud can offer children a unique sense of feeling and engagement with a poem. As Donald Graves (1992: 9) reflects, 'The sound of the voice follows the meaning and thus interprets to others the richness of the language and the subject of the writing'.

The National Literacy Trust survey, *Children, Young People and Poetry* (2018), found that children are engaging with poetry in a wide variety of forms in the digital age. Whilst the majority (87.6%) found poetry in books, almost three quarters of those surveyed listened to poetry (78.2%), found poetry online (74.4%) and nearly two-thirds watched it (61.6%). Watching video performances or listening to audio performances gives children the opportunity to hear and see a wide range of poets reading and performing their poetry. CLPE's 'Poetryline' website and the Children's Poetry Archive have a fantastic selection of video and audio recordings to draw on.

Watching poets perform their poems opens up children's perceptions about poetry, helping them to see the universality of poetry and its relevance to their own lives. It is important to make sure that children have access to the work of a wide range of poets, and to the work of poets that reflect the realities of children in our schools. One teacher on CLPE's Power of Poetry project reflected on how she had shared Valerie Bloom's 'Haircut Rap' video on Poetryline with her children. A child in the class remarked,' I didn't know poets can be black people too. I thought Valerie Bloom was white'.

Opportunities to hear a range of dialects such as in the poetry of Valerie Bloom, Grace Nichols, James Berry and John Agard allow children to see a range of voices and history through poetry. New forms that directly speak to children's own interests such as the hip-hop lyricism of Karl Nova, in his award-winning collection *Rhythm and Poetry*, can entice children not only to perform but also to write from their own experience in ways that directly appeal to them.

PERFORMING POETRY THEMSELVES

Poetry is rooted in word games, wordplay, song and rhythm, and it is particularly important that children have opportunities to enjoy reading poetry aloud themselves, joining in, dramatising and performing poems. If poetry is not given a voice, if it just stays on the page as a printed object, then it is not going to come alive for most children. As Debbie Pullinger (2017: 67) states, 'A poem is an invitation to inhabit the voice of the poem and to give it voice … to feel the full effects we have to speak it, to fill it with our breath, shape it in our mouths and feel it in our bodies'.

Before performing, children will need to explore and become familiar with their chosen poem.

When the children have made a connection with a poem, they can start to look at it in more depth, thinking about how best to convey this connection to their audience. They can think about whether the poem works best performed by an individual, a pair or a group, as well as how they will use their voices to build emotion and understanding. Supporting children to work up performances of poems is a fantastic way of improving reading fluency, encouraging them to read and re-read, note how the punctuation guides reading, and work out where to pause to enhance the emotion and meaning.

READING AND RESPONDING TO POETRY

Children need time to read, re-read and respond to poetry, to internalise and respond to it at a personal level.

A technique like 'poetry papering' works really well. Select a number of different poems, illustrating various poets, styles and forms. Photocopy the poems and pin them up around the classroom or another space for the children to find and explore at their leisure. They can read, pass over, move on and then select one they'd like to talk about with someone else. This encourages the children to enjoy the experience of simply reading a poem, to relish the uncertainties of meanings and the nature of the knowledge and emotional responses that poems invoke in them as readers. Let them look for connections, ask questions, explore what they like about poems and the use of language.

Children can then go on to re-read the poem and explore it in greater depth, in pairs or small groups. They might start by thinking about what the poem says to them, the personal connections they have with it or what questions it poses for them. Sometimes, poetry can be viewed as an easy option, or not giving enough for children to develop real reading stamina as there are often fewer words on the page and far more white space than a short story or novel. Far from being easy, the brevity of the words on the page, the presence of the white space, the line and verse breaks, how words are arranged on the page all provide opportunities for the investigation of authorial choices and allow children to reflect and consider deeply. As Michael Rosen (2011: 21) surmises, poetry 'frequently asks questions, suggests thoughts, offers possibilities and tackles ideas. It often does this without closing off the matter in hand, or wrapping things up with neat conclusions. As a consequence, poetry leaves gaps for readers thinking and opens up many areas for thought and discussion'. Children need time and space to engage in authentic dialogue about poems, facilitated by supportive adults who can intervene where necessary to pick up or extend discussions with enabling questions.

You can then go on to revisit poems that children have an interest in and use these as an opportunity to introduce them to the names of specific forms or devices, looking at how poets have crafted words to evoke their thoughts and feelings. You might introduce this by way of what Michael Rosen (2016) calls 'secret strings'. He talks about the importance of discovering how the poet might have used assonance, alliteration, imagery, rhythm and sound, and what this evokes in the reader as they read. In this way, poetry is a wonderful vehicle for focusing on and discussing author intent, which serves well for the kinds of higher-level questions children may meet in tests and on essay questions in Key Stages 3 and 4.

USING POETRY TO SUPPORT READING AND SPELLING SKILLS AND !

Poetry is many children's route into reading. Its rhythms and patterns introduce children to a range of reading skills. Children naturally pick up rhymes and rhythms, they want to join in, they enjoy the experience, and a rich experience of hearing and learning poems is a fantastic way of learning how language works. Wordplay is one of the most basic pleasures of poetry, giving the opportunity for playing games with language so that the shapes, sounds, and rhythms of words are enjoyed as well as their meaning.

Encourage children to play with song, rhyme and verse throughout the primary years. Support them in hearing the pulse and syllabic beats in poems; look at rhyme patterns in poetry and link this to children's understanding of onset and rime, developing their knowledge of how words look and are spelt.

Poetry also gives an invitation for children to play with words. Many poems contain 'nonsense words', which are a key feature of the current Phonic Screening Check. Exploring such words in the context of a familiar poem allows children to investigate how these are used and how we read their meaning in the context of the poem. One of the best examples of this for young children is Michael Rosen's *Once*, which begins:

Once upon a plom
There lived a poor little mom
Along with her children three.
There was a great big Gom
A Flom and a Chom
Who all sang, "Me, me, me."

Then the Flom saig "Ping!"
And the Chom said, "Ting!"
And the Gom said, "Ping Pong Pee."
And the poor little mom
Said to the Gom,
"What about me, me, me?"

(From *A Great Big Cuddle* by Michael Rosen, illustrated by Chris Riddell (Walker))

Children will need to use their knowledge of phonics to allow them to decode these unfamiliar words, but will also need to acknowledge that the words have meaning in the context of the poem, thinking about who these characters are, what they are like and the relationships between them. One of the problems with the Rose Review stating that 'teaching relatively short, discrete daily sessions, designed to progress from simple elements to the more complex aspects of phonic knowledge, skills and understanding' is that phonics is anything but discrete. It is part of the knowledge that allows us to become fluent and successful readers.

As children's knowledge of word structures develops, rhyming poetry is an excellent way of contextualising work around the variations in the English spelling system. A poem with rhyming couplets, such as Roger McGough's 'The Lost-Lost Property Office', allows children to be supported in their reading by the rhyme patterns and they can explore the different rime patterns in the words and the similarities and differences in how they are spelt, e.g.:

Believe/leave, hot/not, slowly/goalie, ballerina/concertina, say/grey, suit/parachute

A poem such as this one can lead into a contextualised investigation into spelling, spelling rules and patterns and a developing understanding of onset and rime.

For more experienced readers, poetry is an excellent tool for looking at the complexities of the spelling system. Joseph Coelho's 'The Duelling Duo', from *Overheard in a Tower Block*, contains a wealth of homophones that children can read and discuss to consider the deeper meanings behind the poem for example:

Each trying to raze

the other to the ground,

ignoring the sun's rays,

they danced their iron,

refusing to pause,

ignoring the sweat,

that rained from their pores,

each desperate to reign

with their armour-bash peel.

EXAMPLES OF SUPPORTIVE TEXTS FOR READERS ACROSS THE PRIMARY YEARS

Single poet collections enable children to gain a window into a poet's style, range and inspirations over the course of a collection. When selecting collections for the classroom, look for and make available those which allow the opportunity to open children's eyes to what poetry is and what it can do. Such collections will have within them humorous poems, lyrical poems that follow rich rhythms, emotive poetry written from personal experience, and poems that offer windows into the writer's fascinations and direct, real-life experience.

Carefully collected anthologies allow children to experience a wide range of poets and voices in one book. Some anthologies are arranged in themes so that children can easily find poems that link to areas of interest.

WHAT IS IMPORTANT IN THE EARLY YEARS?

- Playing with words and language.
- A focus on rhythm and rhyme, including links with early phonological development.
- Encouraging early readers to join in and perform.
- Varied collections that allow children to also emotionally engage with texts, to see themselves and their experiences reflected.

For Early Years, one of the best collections of recent years is *A Great Big Cuddle* by Michael Rosen, illustrated by Chris Riddell (Walker Books). Poems like 'Tippy-Tappy' and

'The Button Bop' allow children to explore and experiment with the sounds of language and recognising alliteration – essential precursors to forming, articulating and recognising speech sounds – and showing children that language can be fun, playful and experimental. Others like 'Music' and 'Bendy Man' introduce a focus on the rhythm and lyricism of poetry, encouraging children to chime in with repeated phrases and patterns, engaging with the language they hear and say and moving physically to poetry, feeling the rhythm in their bodies and building the foundations for writing, drawing and counting. The potential for poetry to be a creative form of expression can be seen in poems such as 'I Am Angry, Let Me Do It' and 'Lost' where personal narrative and the expression of emotion can be seen and recognised. This allows children a window into self-reflection; teachers can facilitate open discussions around the poems that allow children to make personal connections with their own emotions and experiences and those of others, supporting their personal, social and emotional development alongside their early literacy skills and knowledge.

Our first experiences of poetry are often through song and rhyme. The musicality of James Carter's poetry in *Zim Zam Zoom*, illustrated by Nicola Colton, is perfect for the Early Years, inviting children to chime in with repeated words and refrains in poems such as the title poem 'Zim Zam Zoom!' and 'Yumtime!', and giving them the opportunity to use their voices to explore sounds ('Firework Poem' and 'Hullabaloo').

Anthologies such as *Here's a Little Poem*, edited by Jane Yolen and Andrew Fusek Peters and illustrated by Polly Dunbar (Walker), provide a broad range of poems and voices that connect to children's everyday realities, experiences and emotions. The importance of links to the outdoors is made in the *I Go Outside* section, with traditional poems like Robert Louis Stevenson's 'The Swing' sitting alongside new modern classics like Tony Mitton's 'Rickety Train Ride'.

WHAT IS IMPORTANT IN KS1

- Continued exploration of language and vocabulary, texts that allow the developing reader to take control of the reading.
- Collections which showcase the variety of what poetry is and what it can do, from the wildly humorous to the reflective and emotional.
- Poems and collections that allow children to see themselves, topics and themes of interest to them, e.g. nature, their immediate environment, reflective experiences from home or school.

Shirley Hughes' *Out and About* (Walker Books) contains poems themed around children's direct experiences with the outdoor environment, supporting their vocabulary and talk and providing language models and structures for them to articulate their own ideas and experiences.

How to be a Tiger by George Szirtes is an excellent example of a single poet collection for this age-range. The collection shows children a broad range of poetry and offers insights into different themes, styles and forms, moving between poems that are descriptive to humourous to contemplative.

Thinker: My Puppy Poet and Me by Eloise Greenfield and illustrated by Ehsan Abdollahi (Tiny Owl) is a wonderful and unique collection which showcases a range of poetic forms. It is almost a verse novel, made up of poems about a young boy, Jace, and his dog, Thinker. The exploration of Jace's world through poems about his everyday environment, combined with rich and inviting illustrations of a child's everyday world, are an open invite for children to discuss their own lives and likes in relation to the poems, and provide an excellent invitation for children to write about their own experiences.

WHAT IS IMPORTANT IN KS2

- Poems that show children the full variety of what poetry is and what it can do for them both as readers and as writers.
- Exploring a wide range of dialects and voices.
- Different forms and styles that reflect the rhythm and lyricism of poetry.
- Exploring a wide range of poetic forms and how and why these are used.
- Sophistication in humour and wordplay.
- Poems that evoke deeper responses; emotional, social issues, political.
- Links with wordplay and spelling.
- Exploring the history of influential poets from the past and how this influences present day poetry.
- Longer narrative poems and verse novels to build reading stamina.

Things You Find in a Poet's Beard by A.F. Harrold is a perfect Key Stage 2 collection with a mix of themes and poetic forms that will delight and inspire young readers and writers. Everyday objects such as a Jammie Dodger in *Jam* or the 'humble sock' in *Socks*, provide starting points for children's own funny poems. The humour and wordplay in poems such as 'The Warning' and 'Two Quick Tips' encourage children to look at the meanings of words, as well as providing belly laughs. Quieter poems such as 'The Taste of a Biscuit' and 'A Poem for My Mum' enable children to respond emotionally to poems as well as showing them that writing poetry can be a cathartic experience, helping them vocalise and make sense of their own emotions.

In *Moon Juice*, Kate Wakeling's musicality flows throughout the poems showing a consistent sensitivity to the rhythm and power of language. There is a range of subject matter, style and form and themes ranging from the familiar to the traditional and fantastic. Poems like 'Comet' beg to be performed, with a direct instruction ('To be read as quickly as possible, in as few breaths as you can manage') and there are also poems like 'New Moon' and 'Jungle Cat' with excellent examples of rich and descriptive language used to draw a reader into an experience.

As children grow with poetry, they learn that it can be a vehicle for communicating a message or opinion. John Agard is a master of this in his poetry. Never patronising to his audience, his voice is powerful yet subtle, and encourages a deeper level of thought and discussion. *The Rainmaker Danced* contains rich and lyrical poems, set against striking illustrations by Satoshi Kitamura, that invite us to consider our own impact on each other and the environment.

THE READER IN THE WRITER

Immersing children in the pleasures of poetry, through listening to, reading, responding to and performing a wide range of poetry, supports children to understand that poetry is a powerful form of creative expression and provides them with models – and choices – about how they write poetry for themselves.

> "IMMERSING CHILDREN IN THE PLEASURES OF POETRY, THROUGH LISTENING TO, READING, RESPONDING TO AND PERFORMING A WIDE RANGE OF POETRY, SUPPORTS CHILDREN TO UNDERSTAND THAT POETRY IS A POWERFUL FORM OF CREATIVE EXPRESSION."

If children have experienced a range of poetry, they then have a context to discover the rich history of poetry, exploring where these forms came from and how they work as well as showing them what they can do in their own writing. Giving children personal writing journals that they have control over sharing allows them to collect and try out personal ideas before sharing them with a wider audience. Some forms may have 'rules' but poetry allows you to break those rules – with layout, with punctuation, with style.

In our work with schools and children, we have seen many examples of children gaining a sense of voice and choice in their writing through creating poetry of their own. In writing poetry children are encouraged to reflect on their experience, to recreate it, shape it, and make sense of it. In a poem it is possible to give form and significance to a particular event or feeling and communicate this to the reader or to the listener.

Poems studied can evoke feelings in children that inspire them to write poems of their own. In the example below, Mahir, a 10-year-old boy from London, wrote a unique response after hearing the poem 'Gingerbread Man' by Joseph Coelho. The original poem by Coelho shares the sense of guilt and shame experienced by the 'I' in the poem, reflecting back on a playground experience of bullying:

GINGERBREAD MAN

Billy chased me round the playground
with hands full of fists.

Billy yelled at me across the football pitch
with a mouth full of stings.

Billy spat, jibed and cawed
as I ran away singing …

"You can't catch me, I'm the Gingerbread man."

Billy had red hair.
I was cruel and called him names.

(From *Werewolf Club Rules* by Joseph Coelho (Frances Lincoln, 2014))

Mahir's poem in response evokes the original theme of bullying and switches in mood from the anger expressed in the first verse to the shame the writer is left with at the end of the poem, but he has made the poem his own, not just substituted words. He wrote after responding to the poem as it was these themes and emotions that spoke to him directly and resonated with experiences of his own, and he felt inspired to write in his own voice to make sense of his own experiences. In his response to his own poem, Mahir commented, 'I wrote this poem because I was experiencing people calling me black and a terrorist so I wrote this poem for other people who is getting threatened or who is getting called terrorist, so I wrote this poem to the bully'.

RACISM

They called me black
but I said don't
We have the same blood.
They called me a terrorist
but I worship Allah and I will prove you wrong.

I was full of red
And I hit them
I was angry
And I left a mark.
I was ashamed.

When children are exposed to a range of poets and poetry, when they understand what poetry is for and can do and they can begin to find their own voices through writing poetry such as this, we discover as teachers its true power.

REFERENCES

Camden, S. (2019) *What advice would you give on performing poetry?* CLPE Poetryline, https://clpe.org.uk/poetryline/interviews/steven-camden

Graves, D.H. (1992) *Explore Poetry*. London: Heinemann Educational Books.

Lambirth, A. (2017) *Evaluation of the Centre for Literacy in Primary Education (CLPE) Power of Poetry Training Programme Final Report, July 2017*. London: CLPE.

Primary National Strategy (2006) *Phonics and early reading: an overview for headteachers, literacy leaders and teachers in schools, and managers and practitioners in Early Years settings*. London: DfES.

Pullinger, D. (2017) *From Tongue to Text: A New Reading of Children's Poetry*. London: Bloomsbury.

Rosen, M. (2011) 'Reflections on Being Children's Laureate – And Beyond', in M. Lockwood (ed.), *Bringing Poetry Alive*. London: Sage.

Rosen, M. (2016) *What is Poetry? The Essential Guide to Reading & Writing Poems*. London: Walker.

The National Literacy Trust (2018) *Children, Young People and Poetry in 2018*. London: National Literacy Trust.

FIND OUT MORE

Andrews, R. (1991) *The Problem with Poetry*. Milton Keynes: Open University Press.

Bryan, B. and Styles, M. (eds) (2013) *Teaching Caribbean Poetry*. Abingdon: Routledge.

CLPE Poetryline https://clpe.org.uk/poetryline

CLPE (2018) *Poetry in Primary Schools: What We Know Works*. https://clpe.org.uk/library-and-resources/research/poetry-what-we-know-works

Dymoke, S., Lambirth, A. and Wilson, A. (eds) (2013) *Making Poetry Matter*. London: Bloomsbury.

Dymoke, S., Lambirth, A. and Wilson, A. (eds) (2014) *Making Poetry Happen*. London: Bloomsbury.

Rosen, M. (1989) *Did I Hear You Write?* Nottingham: Five Leaves.

Sedgwick, F (1997) *Read my Mind*. Abingdon: Routledge.

The Children's Poetry Archive https://childrens.poetryarchive.org/

Watts, A. (2017) *Exploring Poetry with Young Children*. London: David Fulton.

CHILDREN'S POETRY BOOKS REFERENCED IN THIS CHAPTER

Agard, J. and Kitamura, S. (2017) *The Rainmaker Danced*. London: Hodder.

Carter, J. and Colton, N. (2016) *Zim Zam Zoom*. London: Otter Barry Books.

Coelho, J. (2014) *Werewolf Club Rules*. London: Frances Lincoln.

Coelho, J. (2017) *Overheard in a Tower Block*. London: Otter Barry Books.

Greenfield, E. and Abdollahi, E. (2018) *Thinker, My Puppy Poet and Me*. London: Tiny Owl.

Harrold, A.F. and Riddell, C. (2015) *Things You Find in a Poet's Beard*. Portishead: Burning Eye.

Henderson, K. (2013) *The Dragon With A Big Nose*. London: Frances Lincoln.

Hughes, S. (2015) *Out and About: A First Book of Poems*. London: Walker.

McGough, R. (2015) *Poetry Pie*. London: Puffin

Nova, K. (2017) *Rhythm and Poetry*. Keighly: Caboodle Books.

Rosen, M. and Riddell, C. (2015) *A Great Big Cuddle*. London: Walker.

Wakeling, K. and Braslina, E. (2016) *Moon Juice*. Birmingham: The Emma Press.

Yolen, J. and Fusek Peters, A. (eds) (2007) *Here's a Little Poem*. London: Walker.

CHAPTER 6

PICTUREBOOKS IN THE PRIMARY SCHOOL

CHARLOTTE HACKING

Picturebooks offer a special and unique reading experience, using words and pictures together to draw the reader in and immersing them in the narrative. As Barbara Bader (1976: 1) defines it, 'A picturebook is text, illustrations, total design; an item of manufacture and a commercial product; a social, cultural, historic document; and foremost, an experience for a child. As an art form it hinges on the interdependence of pictures and words, on the simultaneous display of two facing pages, and on the drama of the turning page'.

At the Centre for Literacy in Primary Education, we have conducted a six-year study (2013–2019) into how picturebooks are being used across the primary years and how children of all ages view them as part of a broad, rich reading experience.

Although some children in our study already knew the value of picturebooks for children of all ages to support a breadth and range of reading experience, the vast majority of the children questioned saw picturebooks as a step into reading or a support for less able readers:

'Picturebooks are for people that can't really read that's why the pictures are there to give them an idea what the book is about'.

'They are for everyone but mostly little children and children who find other books challenging – because the people who can't read can look at the pictures'.

'They're for little children who are starting to read – so younger children can develop the reading skills before reading chapter books'.

This is unsurprising in the current educational climate. In December 2018, the DFE produced a series of video excerpts to exemplify reading assessment at Key Stage 1. The children working 'at the expected standard', are shown predominantly reading picturebooks, with the introduction of a short novel, showing a breadth of reading for this age group. However, the video exemplification for the children 'reading at greater depth within the expected standard' shows all of them reading short stories or longer novels, such as Roald Dahl's *George's Marvellous Medicine*, *The Beginning of the Armadillos* by Rudyard Kipling and J.K. Rowling's *Harry Potter and the Goblet of Fire*.

However, we know from our research that picturebooks are an important genre of children's literature and not just a step on the route to chapter books.

"WE KNOW FROM OUR RESEARCH THAT PICTUREBOOKS ARE AN IMPORTANT GENRE OF CHILDREN'S LITERATURE AND NOT JUST A STEP ON THE ROUTE TO CHAPTER BOOKS."

They support the development of sophisticated reading skills, enabling children to develop deep comprehension skills and to learn about narrative structure and character development in an accessible way:

Good picturebooks are not trite, simple or juvenile. Picturebooks today cover a range of topics that have universal significance: sibling rivalry, time passing, war, nuclear holocaust, death and a variety of political statements. Picturebooks offer humour, irony, poetry, good stories well told, social criticism and deep psychological insights. Moreover, they offer readers ways of 'getting into the story' by 'wandering around inside the picture'. (Michaels and Walsh, 1990: 4)

The importance of the visual alongside the verbal in picturebooks supports an emotional engagement with a story. We can actually see characters' emotions and reactions and the colour choices and perspectives are all designed to encourage us to look at events in the story in a certain way. As Maria Nikolajeva (2014: 99) observes, 'picturebooks offer a whole new dimension of cognitive and affective challenges to novice readers' – a dimension of challenge that we, as educators, must never dismiss or underestimate.

CHOOSING AND USING PICTUREBOOKS ACROSS THE PRIMARY SCHOOL

So, how do we know what constitutes a high-quality picturebook and what should we look for when selecting texts to use with children at different ages and stages?

Many of the best picturebooks, those that are rich and multilayered, will work for readers of all ages. With a greater life experience and knowledge and understanding of the world, children will see more in the text as a whole and understand at greater depth the themes and ideas contained within. Even a text as simple as David McKee's *Not Now Bernard*, can be observed in a different light by older children. On re-reading the text in Year 6, Jay-Shaun surmised, 'there's not actually a monster at all! It's like when my mum calls my brother a little monster when he's being naughty, it's just that Bernard is acting up because his mum and dad are ignoring him'. This is an idea that simply wouldn't have occurred to him on first reading the text in Reception.

Croc and Bird by Alexis Deacon is a text that can work in this way. Croc and Bird hatch out from eggs lying side by side on the sand and assume that they are brothers. They nurture and shelter each other but the day comes when they realise that they are not brothers after all. Younger children understand the concepts of making friends, shared experiences and learning to get along with each other. Older children will be able to look at the nuances involved in a crocodile and a bird thinking they were brothers and how this relates to their wider life experiences. A teacher on the research project observed her Year 5 class at the point where Croc and Bird are faced with the discovery that they aren't actually brothers at all:

'The impact of the double-page spread was enormous. With no words on the page, the children gasped and began to chat immediately. Conversations were all about Croc and Bird ... Discussions about gender – 'brothers', talk about family, being alone, nature/ nurture, being forced to make choices, being depressed, anxious and lonely'.

As well as planning to use some picturebooks across the primary school, it is also important to consider creating a 'spine' of picturebooks to support children's developing understanding of creating meaning through verbal and visual cues.

PICTUREBOOKS FOR CHILDREN IN THE EARLY YEARS

Picturebooks are the perfect introduction to reading for children. They help children understand that meaning can be made through the text on the page and the images they see. The smaller amounts of text on the page allow them to practise core skills, such as 1:1 correspondence, recognition of common words and reading to punctuation.

Oh No George! by Chris Haughton offers young readers the perfect introduction to the joys and delights of the picturebook. Bold, striking colours draw the attention and readers are introduced to the protagonist, George, on the front cover with a full-face portrait. As the narrative unfolds, George has to take responsibility for his own actions as Harris leaves him alone. In the Early Years, children will be learning how to self-regulate and will be able to directly relate to George's struggles. Each time he's facing temptation, we are shown a spread replicating the front cover illustration, with the rhetorical question 'What will George do?' This draws the reader into the narrative and makes them part of it. The delight of the page turn, with its shock and humour as we see George drawn to temptation, keeps young readers captivated.

I said I'd be good.
George thinks.
I hoped I'd be good.
but I wasn't.

What will George do?

Figure 6.1

This book also teaches young children a lot about story structure. At the beginning, we are introduced to the characters of George and Harris and the setting, their home. We learn about pacing the narrative, using a pattern of three temptations before we get to the crux of the story – Harris coming home and finding out that George has, in fact, not been good. The 'What will George do?' questions are perfect for opening up a reader response, allowing children to empathise, drawing on personal experience to talk about ways in which the story can be resolved.

The simple text, with its repetitive structure and patterned language, is perfect for encouraging the youngest readers to chime in, begin to recognise that print and pictures carry meaning, and to start to recognise words that often appear in familiar texts.

In the Early Years, where children are developing a wider sense of self, it is important for them to be able to see themselves in stories and respond to stories using their personal experience to develop comprehension.

"IN THE EARLY YEARS, WHERE CHILDREN ARE DEVELOPING A WIDER SENSE OF SELF, IT IS IMPORTANT FOR THEM TO BE ABLE TO SEE THEMSELVES IN STORIES AND RESPOND TO STORIES USING THEIR PERSONAL EXPERIENCE TO DEVELOP COMPREHENSION."

Hello, Friend! by Rebecca Cobb is a perfect example of a story that revolves around protagonists children can relate to and empathise with. Right from the familiar settings on the front cover and endpapers we can begin to see and explore the feelings and reactions of the two main characters.

Figure 6.2

A good quality text should also inspire a focus on children learning more about themselves and the world around them. This text, with its focus on learning how to relate to others and making friends in the context of school, fits perfectly into children's direct experiences at this age. As the rest of the story unfolds, the simple text, with plenty of common words for children to explore and recognise, is told from just one character's point of view. Our sense of the other character's perspective comes from being able to read the illustrations. (More on this specific skill can be found in Chapter 9.) The mix of large, double-page spreads and small vignettes allows us to see the relationship developing and to hypothesise about different perspectives in the story. The illustrations are an invitation for children to discuss, predict and speculate, developing their skills of group discussion and comprehension.

PICTUREBOOKS FOR READERS IN KEY STAGE 1

As children gain more experience and confidence in reading, they will enjoy picturebooks that offer different and varied illustration styles and techniques and storylines that allow them to think more deeply about themselves and the world around them. These texts will allow them to develop greater fluency in reading as they read and re-read to connect the meaning in the words and illustrations and gain a deeper understanding of characters, themes and story concepts.

Lauren Child's, postmodern style, plays with the conventional boundaries of picturebook formats and experiments with type, offering much to delight the developing reader. *The New Small Person* provides opportunities for children to use their own lives and experiences to deeply reflect on the experiences of the main character, Elmore Green.

The new person was small and didn't do much but still people picked it up and smiled at it and gave it things to chew.

They all seemed to like it . . .

maybe
a little bit
MORE
than
they
liked

Somebody else came along.

Elmore Green.

Figure 6.3

Child's mixed-media approach invites us to look more deeply at the illustrations, working out how they have been created and noticing the differences between real and drawn textures. The storytelling in the illustration takes everything from a child's perspective, seeing adults from knee level, and their distinctive simplicity reflects the childlike nature of the subject matter as well as being an invitation for children to have a go themselves. The simplicity of the backgrounds in the story draws our attention to the relationships between the characters, allowing Key Stage 1 children to relate to their own life experience and reflect on what they know about emotions such as jealousy, routine and attachment to personal objects.

The layout and typography take the developing reader into understanding the different ways that text can work on the page. Size of text, layout of lines, use of capitalisation and spacing on the page draw children's attention to the words. These techniques place a different emphasis on parts of text, deepening our understanding of the story and the relationships between the text and illustration in the storytelling.

Beegu, by Alexis Deacon, is a perfect picturebook for developing readers in Key Stage 1. Our relationship with the main character is built from the cover image, with the abstract character set front and centre in a familiar setting. We wonder why this character is here, whether they are lost and how they must be feeling. This is heightened when, on the first page, we have this confirmed by the text: 'Beegu was not supposed to be here. She was lost'. Just how lost she is becomes clear when we look back at the endpapers – a dark sky, full of stars – and the title page – where we see the wreckage of her craft. Re-reading and looking back through the pages of picturebooks is crucial; sometimes later information will encourage us to see more detail in previous images and support the emergence of further layers of understanding.

As the text progresses, Deacon uses more sophisticated techniques to deepen our empathy. Handwritten speech bubbles show that Beegu speaks a different language, and framing is used to show the passing of time, enhancing our understanding of her loneliness. The facial expressions and body positions of the adults she meets show us just how ostracised she is. These are in contrast to the soft vignettes used to emphasise the safe relationships she forges with the children in the book. Although Beegu speaks a different language, we learn about her feelings through the portrayal of her body language, particularly the placement of her ears.

didn't like being alone.

She needed to find some friends.

Figure 6.4

There is much in this text to discuss with children and they can relate to the themes of loneliness, security, how we treat others who may appear different to ourselves, and the importance of family through their own personal experiences and their wider knowledge of current affairs.

PICTUREBOOKS FOR READERS IN KEY STAGE 2

Many picturebooks are deliberately designed for older readers, exploring more complex themes and emotions and requiring a greater life experience to fully comprehend and appreciate the story. Such texts should be a central part of the reading experience in Key Stage 2. Close reading of pictures should continue to be taught and discussions around illustrations as well as text planned regularly into the reading curriculum.

A deceptively complex text for Key Stage 2 readers is *Red and the City* by Marie Voigt. From the front cover, the illustrative style, familiar traditional story character and childlike typography may suggest the book is for a younger reader, but the story itself contains complex themes and ideas that require the understanding of an older reader, and children need an understanding of the original Red Riding Hood tale to make sense of this contemporary re-telling.

The limited colour palette of black, white, grey, pink and red will support discussion about mood and effect and what this makes them think about the text. The illustration on the title page almost breaks the 4th wall with the reader, as it suggests she's aware of the title being there, creating opportunities for discussions around the impact of this device and what it suggests about the characters.

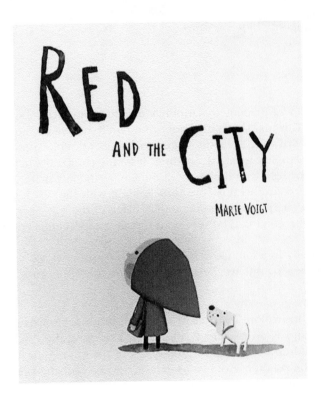

Figure 6.5

As they move through the story, noticing more and more wolf imagery throughout the illustrations, children can talk about and discuss what the wolf represents in this story. They can also explore the character of Woody the Dog and the differences between his reactions to the city compared with Red's. The complexity of the illustrations is juxtaposed with a very simple text, mirroring that of a traditional tale for much younger children. After reading, older readers will be able to discuss more complex ideas around the story: what they think this story was really about; whether there really was a wolf; what they thought the writer wanted to represent with the idea of the wolf; how the story remained true to the original idea of Little Red Riding Hood and what gave this traditional story a modern twist, and whether they thought this brings the story to life for a new generation of readers.

Figure 6.6

Complex themes can be presented alarmingly effectively in picturebooks, as in *The Journey* by Francesca Sanna. This text shares the story of a family whose comfortable, everyday life is destroyed by the onset of war. The story begins on the first double-spread with a family beach scene, which will be familiar to many children. It is this choice of such a familiar scene that will help children empathise with the plight of the family, the fact that this could be any family, anywhere. The use of colour in this spread is striking, with the warm yellows, oranges, reds and green contrasting sharply with the deep, flat, black of the sea – serving as a warning that something dark may be coming. The text on the page supports this contrast:

'I live with my family in a city close to the sea. Every summer we used to spend many weekends at the beach. But we never go there anymore, because last year, our lives changed forever …'

This text offers much to explore in terms of how the authorial choices guide our understanding of the narrative and is an excellent vehicle for exploring the effective use of grammar and punctuation. Children could explore the effect of the change from the present tense in the first sentence to the past tense of 'we used to' in the second, the pragmatic choice of 'But' to begin the third sentence to emphasise this change, and the use of ellipsis at the end to leave the reader to think about what this change might be.

Figure 6.7

As the story continues, the next spreads show hands emerging from the flat black colour, smashing the beach scene, until in the third spread this colour takes over the whole page, emphasising the few objects left behind, including the father's glasses, as we are told very simply 'And one day the war took my father'; the space on the page emphasises this loss and urges the reader to stop and reflect.

The beauty of this book is that it does not sugar-coat the experience; the loss, the complexity of the decision to leave and the difficulty and risk of the journey the family makes are played out thoughtfully and effectively in the words and images. The loss of their personal effects and the danger of them being discovered are also emphasised as the journey progresses. Scale is used to show the dominance of the guard and mirrored spreads with contrasting colours highlight the struggle of the mother.

The ending is hopeful but realistic and does not seek to tie up the story in a happily-ever-after, or provide a saviour to rescue the family. This gives much for older children to discuss in the current climate about the very real situations families face in the onslaught of war, and how such families or individuals may be presented in the media.

Figure 6.8

PLANNING PURPOSEFUL ENGAGEMENTS WITH PICTUREBOOKS IN THE CLASSROOM

All too often picturebooks can be seen as a quick and easy way of sharing a story in the classroom but it is important to plan regular opportunities to explore them deeply. Such opportunities should include the following.

CLOSE READING OF WELL-CHOSEN PICTUREBOOKS

Children need to be taught the language of pictures to be able to discuss the techniques illustrators use in their storytelling. Chapter 9 explores this more deeply, but children can be shown how illustrators communicate using elements such as colour, facial expression, body position, scale, perspective and composition to introduce deeper layers of meaning. When teachers understand how words and pictures are used together to communicate meaning, this helps them to pass this learning on to children, developing deeper comprehension skills and providing additional opportunities to infer, deduce, think critically, empathise and make personal connections within and across texts and real-life experiences.

TIME FOR READING AND RE-READING PICTUREBOOKS

To fully appreciate the complexities of a quality picturebook it is important to plan time for multiple readings. As Jane Doonan (1993: 18) notes, the first reading will bring with it 'the compelling curiosity to read on to find out what happens next, but this works against the pictures that would have me stop and search'. Once children have done this, it is important to get them to read the book again and then for a third time, as it is this time, she goes on to explain, that we need to 'read the words and look at the pictures much more slowly, to begin the process of discovering what relationship(s) they have'.

Sometimes re-reading is seen as a negative reading behaviour. Parents have approached me as a teacher with the comment 'but they've had this book already'. But re-reading is a good thing, helping us to notice more detail with each reading and allowing us to discover deeper layers of meaning, the more we understand about the relationship between the words and the pictures.

TIME FOR DISCUSSION AROUND PICTUREBOOKS, INCLUDING OPPORTUNITIES FOR CHILDREN TO ANNOTATE PICTUREBOOK SPREADS

When children are given time and space to explore spreads in depth, they will be able to work together to read deeply and co-construct meaning from their individual perspectives as readers, deepening their understanding of the text as a whole. As Fiona Maine (2015: 23) points out:

> The approach that is taken to start to make sense of a visual image is steeped in the experiences each reader brings with them, whether they are personal, cultural or both. Potentially, this multiplicity of possible meanings might invite more discussion than a written text, suggesting that the use of images in engaging children in text comprehension can support their disposition to search for meaning and explore possibilities. It can also support children to engage with meanings beyond the literal, rather than being satisfied with the successful decoding of words. With the absence of a 'right answer', children are pushed to justify their reasoning and accept alternatives. They must engage in the critical thinking process.

When children have the time, space and opportunity to discuss picturebooks their thinking becomes visible, and teachers can observe and assess understanding of techniques used by authors and illustrators and their understanding of the text as a whole.

OPPORTUNITIES FOR CHILDREN TO ENGAGE IN ILLUSTRATION THEMSELVES

Children are able to understand story elements more deeply if they engage in illustration themselves. Drawing in the style of a text can help us investigate the lines, shapes and patterns an illustrator has used and can tell us more about characters, settings or events. Noticing such things as when rounded and sharp lines have been used, spatial relationships in the composition of spreads or the scale of one element to another, can all unlock deeper understanding about the story as a whole.

The videos on CLPE's Power of Pictures website show illustrators modelling how to draw characters from picturebooks and teach children how they convey meaning through their illustrations. These can be used as a model for children to draw alongside. It is also important that they see teachers modelling drawing and valuing its role in communicating meaning.

A close study of picturebooks in this way, encouraging a focus on the complexity and artistry of these, can challenge perceptions of how picturebooks are viewed by adults and children alike. As this Key Stage 2 teacher reflects:

> 'I had never really considered reading and working with a picturebook at the level I teach [Y5], thinking it would be 'too easy' or not engaging enough as a model for writing. How things changed! A small group of children were a little suspicious (they thought it might be 'for babies'), but in fact they very quickly came around and were amongst the most insightful as the class began to notice the subtle, deeper layers to the text. Focusing on giving time for deep discussion was fabulous, fully engaging and had impact on their comprehension'.

In turn, after a close study of picturebooks, children's perceptions also changed, with many more children seeing these as a valuable reading experience for children of all ages.

> 'I now think they're for older people too because they make reading more fun and help me understand the story better'.

> 'They are for everyone. They help us understand the emotion of the story and the real story'.

This also helps to validate the importance of other types of multimodal texts, which can also be perceived as a 'lesser' form of reading, such as film and comics.

THE READER IN THE WRITER

Picturebooks give an invaluable opportunity for closely investigating story structure, in a much simpler way than drawing out the structure of a novel. They can be read quickly initially and contain a complete narrative showing children how to plan the bigger shapes of a story from start to finish.

Give time and space for children to read, respond to and discuss the themes and structures of different picturebooks. This provides children with a strong understanding of how to construct a compelling narrative in an accessible way, including characterisation, setting, plot, creating empathy, and pacing the story out from start to finish. We can often be driven to give the children tools to support them in structuring a narrative, giving boxes with prompts, a story mountain or encouraging them to create a far too detailed story map from start to finish. Instead, we should be encouraging children to deepen their knowledge of the big shapes of stories, the five or six key events that really guide a story.

"WE CAN OFTEN BE DRIVEN TO GIVE THE CHILDREN TOOLS TO SUPPORT THEM IN STRUCTURING A NARRATIVE. INSTEAD, WE SHOULD BE ENCOURAGING CHILDREN TO DEEPEN THEIR KNOWLEDGE OF THE BIG SHAPES OF STORIES."

Reading a range of picturebooks and breaking these down into these five or six key shapes, then exploring how the narrative is paced out to lead from one event to the next, can teach them much more about how to shape a narrative as a whole and maintain momentum in their writing throughout a story. As this teacher noted:

'We've seen a huge impact on the children's understanding of story structure and them being able to use the same level of detail throughout their story, rather than in traditional writing where the introduction and beginning have a lot of detail and then the rest tails off'.

REFERENCES

Arizpe, E. and Styles, M. (2016) *Children Reading Picturebooks, Interpreting Visual Texts*, 2nd edition. Abingdon: Routledge.

Bader, B. (1976) *American Picturebooks from Noah to the Beast Within*. London: Macmillan.

CLPE (2019) *The Power of Pictures: Summary of findings from the research on the CLPE Power of Pictures Project 2013-19, June 2019*. https://clpe.org.uk/powerofpictures/research

Dahl, R. (1981) *George's Marvellous Medicine*. London: Puffin.

DFE (2016) *KS2 Reading – Working at the Expected Standard*. https://www.youtube.com/user/educationgovuk/videos

DFE (2018) *KS1 English Reading Exemplification – Working at the Expected Standard*. www.gov.uk/government/publications/ks1-english-reading-exemplification-working-at-the-expected-standard

Doonan, J. (1993) *Looking at Pictures in PictureBooks*. Stroud: Thimble Press.

Kipling, R. and Cauley, L.B. (illus.) (1985) *The Beginning of the Armadillos*. London: Thompson Learning.

Maine, F. (2015) *Dialogic Readers: Children Talking and Thinking Together About Visual Texts*. Abingdon: Routledge.

Michaels, W. and Walsh, M. (1990) *Up & Away: Using PictureBooks*. Australia: Oxford University Press.

Nikolajeva, M. (2014) *Reading for Learning: Cognitive Approaches to Children's Literature*. Amsterdam: John Benjamins.

Rowling, J.K. (2000) *Harry Potter and the Goblet of Fire*. London: Bloomsbury.

FIND OUT MORE

CLPE *Power of Pictures* https://clpe.org.uk/powerofpictures

Evans, J. (ed.) (2009) *Talking Beyond the Page: Reading and Responding to Picturebooks*. Abingdon: Routledge.

Evans, J. (ed.) (2015) *Challenging and Controversial Picturebooks*. Abingdon: Routledge.

Kiefer, B.Z. (1995) *The Potential of Picturebooks*. Upper Saddle River, NJ: Prentice Hall.

Marcus, L.S. (2012) *Show Me a Story: Why PictureBooks Matter*. Somerville, MA: Candlewick Press.

Nikolajeva, M. and Scott, C. (2006) *How Picturebooks Work*. Abingdon: Routledge.

Sailsbury, M. (2015) *100 Great Children's Picturebooks*. London: Laurence King.

Sailsbury, M. and Styles, M. (2012) *Children's Picturebooks: The Art of Visual Storytelling*. London: Laurence King.

CHILDREN'S PICTUREBOOKS REFERENCED IN THIS CHAPTER

Child, L. (2014) *The NEW Small Person*. London: Puffin.

Cobb, R. (2019) *Hello, Friend!* London: Macmillan.

Deacon, A. (2003) *Beegu*. London: Red Fox.

Deacon, A. (2013) *Croc and Bird*. London: Red Fox.

Haughton, C. (2012) *Oh No, George!* London: Walker Books.

McKee, D. (1980) *Not Now Bernard*. London: Andersen Press.

Sanna, F. (2016) *The Journey*. London: Flying Eye Books.

Voight, M. (2018) *Red and the City*. Oxford: OUP.

PART 2

ESSENTIAL TEACHING APPROACHES FOR A RICH READING CURRICULUM

CHAPTER 7

THE READING ENVIRONMENT

KATIE MYLES

A well-managed reading environment reflects the value a school community places on the importance of reading for pleasure and developing lifelong readers. Reading environments where books and information about books are displayed attractively, and where browsing, choosing and reading can take place, are therefore a visible way of establishing and promoting a positive ethos around reading for pleasure (Chambers, 2011).

This chapter considers the practical issues teachers and schools face when reviewing book stock and creating reading environments, whether that be individual class book corners, whole school libraries or building wider links with the community. Questions of choosing, purchasing and displaying books are linked to ideas about how reading for pleasure can be promoted most effectively within the school so that children can gain access to texts, see themselves as readers and enjoy all the benefits this brings.

The reading environment is, of course, much more than how the books are displayed and promoted, it is the way in which the environment encourages the engagement of children in the reading process.

"THE READING ENVIRONMENT IS, OF COURSE, MUCH MORE THAN HOW THE BOOKS ARE DISPLAYED AND PROMOTED, IT IS THE WAY IN WHICH THE ENVIRONMENT ENCOURAGES THE ENGAGEMENT OF CHILDREN IN THE READING PROCESS."

The role and attitudes of teachers are therefore key to creating an environment that promotes reading as a socially engaging activity that is valued and encouraged.

BREADTH AND QUALITY OF LITERATURE – KEY THINGS TO TAKE INTO ACCOUNT

In the first instance, it is really important to carefully consider the texts that are available to the children in individual classes and across the school as a whole. As explored in detail within Section 1 of this book, the range of texts made accessible to children should cover a breadth and variety of genres and formats, ensuring children can experience a full and rich range of reading throughout their primary years.

Wherever possible, the school library should be a resource from which adults can choose a variety of high-quality children's literature and a wide range of reading materials. It can serve as a resource bank for broader reading around a subject or for a particular purpose, for example to support a cross-curricular topic. It can also house a teacher reference library.

The classroom library or book corner should have a core collection of texts, including well-known, well-loved titles to which the children and teacher can return again and again, as well as a wide range of books to support the curriculum, and materials to enable children to read more extensively. This will include books that support children learning to read, books that will introduce children to a growing range of literature, and high-quality information texts which are interesting and enjoyable.

The book area is going to be children's main point of reference in any primary classroom. It therefore needs to contain a range of titles, authors and genres that both support the English curriculum and broaden children's repertoire. For more experienced readers, these books should offer an increasingly challenging range of reading material and include: texts that are multi-layered (capable of being read at different levels); books that deal with important themes; books in which language is used in lively, inventive ways; books by skilful and experienced children's writers and illustrators; traditional and contemporary 'classics' of children's literature; stories with different cultural settings; and texts that promote discussion and reflection.

It is important to include books in the class collections that are particularly supportive for children who are still learning to read, at whatever stage of their primary education they are at. These books help children to behave like readers. They may be: memorable texts that feature repetition and encourage predictions; texts within which rhythm and rhyme are important; texts that allow children to practise and apply their phonic knowledge; books with strong story shapes and structures; books with supportive illustrations; books that draw attention to written language and to the ways books work.

You will also want to include a range of information and non-fiction texts in the class collection. These books should be chosen to be quality examples which show children how text and pictures can work together to provide comprehensive information and an enjoyable reading experience.

Make sure your book stock includes texts that positively reflect children's interests and backgrounds. Seek out books that reflect diversity in terms of race and heritage, disability, gender and gender identity, sexual orientation, age, socioeconomic status, religion and culture. As well as choosing books that make children aware of the wider world beyond their immediate sphere. It is particularly important to pay attention to authors who are writing from authentic personal experience and knowledge and to adults in the school community who know other languages or literatures. Children's home languages should be valued right through education; bilingual texts and resources should therefore be provided to meet the language needs of learners supporting proficiency in English and progress in their home language.

HELP AND SUPPORT WITH CHOOSING BOOKS

Busy teachers often need help finding out what books are available and where to get them. Where they exist, school library services are an incredibly useful resource that can often loan books to schools and support with selection and ordering. The local public library is also an invaluable resource that can develop teachers' knowledge of recently published children's literature, as well as providing a core collection of books that teachers can share with their pupils.

Staff could also make occasional visits to teacher centres, museum collections and local bookshops. Teachers can also sign up to mailing lists such as the online magazine *Books for Keeps* which provide book reviews of recent publications. Specialist bookshops and book suppliers can also provide ideas and supply the school's collections.

CLPE's Core Book Collection (www.clpe.org.uk/corebooks) is a free, helpful collection of in-print titles, curated by our librarian and divided into three sections for each age group. The 'Learning to Read' collection has been specially chosen to support the reading of children who are still inexperienced readers or having some difficulty in reading. The 'Literature' collection lists books which can form the basis of your English curriculum and introduces children to a growing range of texts. Information books have their own collection as they often don't fit into either of the other collections. These are high-quality information texts which are interesting and enjoyable and support all aspects of the English and wider curriculum.

ENSURING CHILDREN HAVE CHOICE AND VOICE IN YOUR BOOK AREA

Listen to and respect children's choices while helping them to broaden their reading range. For example, it is important not to dismiss their enjoyment of certain types of books such as those in popular series. These texts can draw children in, provide important reading practice, and encourage them to read for pleasure.

Children can also be easily put off when they feel adults are making judgements about their reading choices, so to help them move forward in their reading, allow them to have a say in the selection of books for the school reading environment. Ensure you gather pupil opinion, and survey the children on the types of books and reading material they would like to have in the class collections and school library, before making any changes to your book stock. Value children's choices by providing systems and processes that will help them select and recommend books to one another and to adults in the classroom.

Ultimately, if children enjoy reading, they will read more frequently and become better readers. And if teachers and those who work in schools know about the best children's literature available, they will be able to share that with the children they teach and encourage them to be inspired as readers and motivated to read for themselves.

AUDITING YOUR BOOK STOCK

Auditing your book stock regularly is an important way to ensure that the reading material available to the children in your setting will encourage reading for pleasure. This should happen regularly throughout the school year as children's tastes and preferences change and auditing should therefore involve the pupils as well as the staff.

Questions to consider when auditing the book stock available in your classroom:

- What are the children's reading preferences and literary tastes and are they reflected in the reading materials you have available?
- How is the book stock sourced, sustained, reviewed and replenished?
- Who is involved in the decision-making process?
- Do you have a rolling cycle and systems in place to sustain this?
- Are all the children's needs being met?
- Are different genres represented?
- Are all the school's first/home/community languages represented?
- If children are taking books home, are there enough books to choose from?
- Are there multiple copies of books so children can read together?
- Are there stories in different formats? (for example, big books, audio, digital)
- Are the children's own handmade books included in the collections?
- Is supporting material available such as puppets and props?

CREATING A 'BOOK BUZZ' – HOW DOES THIS SUPPORT READERS?

Enthusiasm for books is caught, not taught. Informal talk about books and reading recommendations between teachers and pupils is the starting point for promoting reading.

"ENTHUSIASM FOR BOOKS IS CAUGHT, NOT TAUGHT. INFORMAL TALK ABOUT BOOKS AND READING RECOMMENDATIONS BETWEEN TEACHERS AND PUPILS IS THE STARTING POINT FOR PROMOTING READING."

Teachers can make the opportunity for such talk by regularly reading aloud to children, encouraging children to make peer recommendations, having an author or illustrator focus within the class reading corner or school library that is changed regularly and by supporting the children to share their opinions about the books they have read.

There is a range of ways to highlight and value books which will create a 'book buzz' in your setting and encourage reading for pleasure. For example, displaying a teacher's 'book of the moment', sharing book trailers at the end of the day or during assembly, displaying book posters in prominent locations around the school, creating a 'Book Hall of Fame' based on the children's favourite books, or a class Top Ten Books of the Year. These can also then be pulled together to form a recommendation list for the next class that you teach.

Utilising Book awards and shadowing schemes can also support reader recommendation and introduce children to books they may not have otherwise encountered. Resources to help you shadow awards are freely available on the CLPE website (https://clpe.org.uk/library-and-resources/celebrating-books-and-special-days).

When you create real enthusiasm about books and reading in your class, the impact is palpable. As one teacher told us, 'The **levels of engagement** within my own class have **dramatically improved** with a much higher percentage of children choosing to spend time reading independently. It is no longer a chore – reading is **something we look forward to** doing every day!' (Power of Reading Teacher, Kirklees).

THE ENABLING ADULT – TEACHERS AS READERS: HOW DOES THIS SUPPORT READERS?

The best way for adults to be able to recommend appropriate books to children which extend and develop their reading is for them to be widely read themselves. Teachers who read widely are able to source and recommend books to suit the interests, tastes and needs of their pupils, and draw on this knowledge to inform book choices and planning. Teachers who have a wide knowledge of children's literature have found that they can also use this knowledge to make recommendations about the 'next' books children might try.

It is also key for teachers to be engaged in reading for pleasure for themselves, as when teachers develop their own experience, preferences and enthusiasms in reading, their personal engagement and reflective involvement as adult readers helps them to be very clear about the nature of reading and the experience of being a reader. This then has an impact on teaching practice (Cremin, 2014).

As well as auditing stock, it is also therefore worth considering auditing your own knowledge of children's literature and encouraging your colleagues to do the same. Consider if you have a broad knowledge of children's literature and if you and your colleagues see yourselves as role models in terms of promoting books and reading.

You may want to join an existing teacher book group such as one of the Open University Reading for Pleasure Groups – or set up one of your own. Other ways to encourage reading amongst staff include having a staff swap bookshelf, displaying 'I am currently reading … ' on classroom doors and staff emails, and to have dedicated reading assemblies. Staff could share their own favourite childhood books with the aim that this is eventually handed over to children.

Encourage staff to share 'recommended reads' at the start of each staff meeting, organise story swap times where teachers read to different year groups on a regular basis, and ask staff to create their own 'Desert Island texts' that they can share with pupils. Support informal free voluntary reading time in the curriculum, such as DEAR (drop everything and read) where the pupils and staff can enjoy uninterrupted reading for pleasure.

READING AREAS: WHAT DO THEY SAY TO READERS IN YOUR CLASSROOM?

When considering the ways in which books are shared, shown and displayed in classrooms and in spaces throughout the school, the question to have at the forefront of your mind is does the environment invite children to read?

All books and reading materials need to be displayed attractively and conveniently. Ensure books are displayed face on to encourage browsing and choosing, and so that children can revisit and interact with the reading materials available. It is often useful to browse book-shops and libraries to see the types of techniques that they use to engage visitors with reading, as many of these can be easily replicated in a classroom reading area. This might be as simple as promoting a 'book of the week' or writing short reviews of the books that can be popped inside the books for readers to discover as they are browsing.

It can be tempting to fill the reading area with a huge amount of books, however often less is more as this ensures that you know the books available and have read them yourself. It also ensures you are supporting the children to learn the skills of browsing and selecting texts and will enable you to rotate stock throughout the year, therefore creating a regular supply of 'new' books for the class to be excited by.

When developing the reading areas in classrooms, it is also essential to ensure you have asked the children what they would like their reading environment to look like, how they would like to read, and how they want to engage with the reading materials available. It is also valuable to engage the pupils in the organisation and maintenance of the books, as this will give you an insight into their preferences and tastes, as well as their ability to differentiate between genres.

Encourage the children to interact with the space by inviting them to share their reader response and reader views; this could be by offering the opportunity to complete their own short reviews or by making recommendations to friends in the class. Ensuring that the children's own written material such as class books and poetry collections are displayed and valued in the reading area, also supports children to see themselves not only as readers but also as writers.

Questions to consider when auditing the reading areas in your setting:

- What do pupils want?
- How are books displayed and categorised?
- Are there categories such as books we know well, easy reads, short novels, poetry, books about animals etc.?
- Do you use labelled baskets or boxes to aid browsing and choosing?
- Is shelving adequate?
- Do you display some books face on?

- Do you create displays with children, e.g. our top ten books, an author display?
- Do you display children's reviews and comments?
- Are there any extras, e.g. cushions, carpet, chairs, plants, drapes, to give a warm comfortable feel?

IMMERSING CHILDREN IN THE TEXT

Many books lend themselves to displays which help children enter the world of the book. Teachers find that building a display or a reading area that piques children's interest or encourages deeper reflection both celebrates the text and also highlights the centrality of the book to the learning that is going on. Teachers who are on the Power of Reading project share their work as part of the course and we see many wonderful examples of practice. From book corners in Andersen Shelters to help children enter the WW2 world of *Tom's Midnight Garden*, to reading in Big Top Tents when studying *Leon and the Place Between*, there are many, many examples of how a reading area can be made the focus area of any classroom.

ACCESS AND TIME: HOW YOU MAKE TIME FOR REAL READING

Of course, in order for children to access the reading environments and the books it is absolutely crucial that there are clear, regular and planned reading routines in place.

Making time for sustained uninterrupted free voluntary reading, such as Everybody Reading In Class – ERIC (Chambers, 2011), should happen every day and for as long as the children can maintain their interest and concentration. This will vary depending on both the age and experience of the children and can be planned to fit around your school day. Do remember though that for it to be seen as a valued time by the children there should be expectations that it happens regularly and for a minimum amount of time – it shouldn't be something that is done purely as a 'filler' and definitely not as a punishment. As defined by Stephen Krashen, this free voluntary reading means 'reading because you want to; no book report; no questions at the end of the chapter; putting down a book you don't like and choosing another one instead; it is the kind of reading highly literate people do all the time' (Krashen, 2004:17).

It is also important to develop a culture of formal and informal book groups throughout the school community to promote engagement in reading, wider discussion skills and inferential understanding. This could be organised and run by reading volunteers and support staff as well as teachers. Our research into book clubs at CLPE (https://clpe.org.uk/library-and-resources/useful-resources/starting-book-group-guide) showed us that there were a number of useful things that help maximise the success of any book group. Allowing the children to choose from a selection of carefully chosen texts also gave them a sense of autonomy. Exploring exciting follow-up activities to hook and keep the children interested and to enhance ideas and understanding of the texts also ensured the club sustained momentum after the first sessions. Picking books in a series was also really effective in encouraging the children to then go on to read the rest of the books in that series. Alex T. Smith's *Claude in the City* (Hodder, 2011) was a particularly popular choice. Investigating ways to support the spread of enthusiasm also ensured the book clubs were sustainable and reached more children. For example, using Year 5 and 6 children as Book Group leaders was a strategy one school used to open up opportunities for keen readers to have their own book clubs. Recognition of the book club's achievements through special assemblies, a special display in a whole school area, or rewarding with attendance certificates or a book token at the end of term, also gave the children pride in what they were doing.

Practical considerations such as picking a time that is convenient for parents, staff and the children themselves are also essential to making sure the book clubs get off the ground and are successful; children will not be encouraged when the club is at football or golden time! Ensure that class teachers are aware of the children's involvement in the club, its aims and ethos so that they can support the work too and can feed in their response to the children's development. We also found that giving the group a special identity, like a special club and allowing the children to choose the name of the club, make pledges to the club members and agree 'rules', helped children feel they were part of something special.

Questions to consider when reviewing the reading routines in your setting:

- Who is accessing the reading area – adults and children?
- Why, how and when are children accessing the area?
- What opportunities are there for children to browse and read together?
- How much opportunity do children have to browse, select, share and discuss books within the classroom?
- How are children supported in accessing, choosing and reading the texts?
- How much time and space are children given to read – individually and together?
- What is the culture of reader recommendation – between the children and by adults?
- How do you know what children are reading? How do the children keep track of what's read?

THE WIDER COMMUNITY: WHY YOU NEED LIBRARIES, VOLUNTEERS, PEER MENTORS, AND THE IMPORTANCE OF FAMILY INVOLVEMENT

It is really important that the invitations to be part of the school reading community involve as many people as possible and include all staff as well as parents and families.

A school library and the way in which this is utilised will ensure pupils enjoy reading and see themselves as readers regardless of their starting points. Wherever possible having dedicated member/s of staff will ensure the library is a well-run space and offers the school further opportunities to build a community of readers. Electing child school librarians to organise and run the library alongside these adults will raise the status of the library and the value your school community places on reading.

The library can provide the means to display new titles to the children, to further support the development of browsing and choosing, to cultivate informal book talk and book gossip, and can be a space in which book groups can be hosted. If you have a school library it is essential that it is a welcoming space and accessible at lunchtime, playtime and if possible before and after school. Children should be able to drop in as well as having a dedicated time to visit the library with their class and teacher so that they can choose books to borrow and take home.

It is also important to harness the power of peer modelling and child reading role models. The children in your setting who can and do read for pleasure and enjoyment will provide the ideal role models for other children.

"IT IS IMPORTANT TO HARNESS THE POWER OF PEER MODELLING AND CHILD READING ROLE MODELS. THE CHILDREN IN YOUR SETTING WHO CAN AND DO READ FOR PLEASURE AND ENJOYMENT WILL PROVIDE THE IDEAL ROLE MODELS FOR OTHER CHILDREN."

Reading across year groups, such as older children reading with younger children on a regular basis, child-led book groups, buddy readers, child librarians and book corner monitors will enable you to support this process.

Developing close links between home and school is essential to developing a culture of reading for pleasure in your school, as it allows all adults around the child to observe and evaluate reading behaviours and preferences. This will then enable teachers to fine-tune the provision of reading materials, support and resources based on the information gleaned.

Reading volunteers and book-related fundraising activities are also ways of involving the wider community and help to create a community of readers. Programmes such as Beanstalk provide fully trained volunteers but you can also encourage parents to volunteer to read with children.

As children mature as readers, they begin to engage with a greater selection of books and texts. It is crucial that the environment around them supports them to take on the multi-faceted reading demands of the curriculum and helps them to widen their reading horizons. A positive, exciting and supportive environment where reading is given prominence and prestige will help them to develop preferences and special interests and experience a personal involvement in reading.

Reading for pleasure often begins as shared pleasures and emotional satisfaction arising from reading with an adult or experienced reader. Provision of a rich reading programme that enables shared experiences and the opportunity to encounter a wide variety of books will ensure the range of personal reading choice grows.

How your reading environment is planned, organised and maintained is therefore absolutely crucial to developing children who can and do read for pleasure, and who will therefore enjoy all the benefits this affords them.

REFERENCES

Chambers, A. (2011) *Tell Me: Children, Reading and Talk with The Reading Environment*. Stroud: The Thimble Press.

CLPE (1991) *The Reading Book*. London: CLPE.

CLPE (2016) *The Reading and Writing Scales*. London: CLPE.

CLPE (2018) *Reading for Pleasure: What We Know Works*. London: CLPE.

CLPE (2018) *Choosing and Using High Quality Texts: What We Know Works*. London: CLPE.

Cremin, T. et al. (2014) *Building Communities of Engaged Readers: Reading for Pleasure*. Abingdon: Routledge.

Krashen, S. (2004) *The Power of Reading*. London: Heinemann. www.researchrichpedagogies.org

FiND OUT MORE

Beanstalk www.beanstalkcharity.org.uk/

Book clubs research – CLPE https://clpe.org.uk/library-and-resources/useful-resources/starting-book-group-guide

Books for Keeps http://booksforkeeps.co.uk/

Book Trust https://www.booktrust.org.uk/

Carousel www.carouselguide.co.uk/

Core Books https://clpe.org.uk/corebooks

Power of Reading website https://clpe.org.uk/powerofreading

Power of Reading, The Literacy Environment https://clpe.org.uk/powerofreading/teaching-approaches/literacy-environment

Schools with Power of Reading subscriptions can access all the audit questions – and more – from the School Library Association www.sla.org.uk/

CHiLDREN'S BOOKS REFERENCED iN THiS CHAPTER

Smith, A.T. (2011) *Claude in the City*. London: Hodder Children's Books.

Pearce, P. and Einzig, S. (2015) *Tom's Midnight Garden*. Oxford: OUP.

McAllister, A. and Baker-Smith, G. (2009) *Leon and the Place Between*. London: Templar.

CHAPTER 8

A READ ALOUD PROGRAMME

FARRAH SERROUKH

The act of reading aloud is instrumental in supporting a child on their road towards becoming a literate being. It therefore needs to be a frequent and routine part of each school day. Reading aloud slows written language down and enables children to hear and take in the distinctive tunes and patterns.

"THE ACT OF READING ALOUD IS INSTRUMENTAL IN SUPPORTING A CHILD ON THEIR ROAD TOWARDS BECOMING A LITERATE BEING."

It temporarily alleviates the weight of having to navigate the text, and frees the child to imagine the scenes and moments portrayed and reflect on the thoughts and feelings that the author seeks to inspire in their readers. Furthermore, it enables children to experience and enjoy stories that they might not otherwise meet. By reading well-chosen books aloud, teachers help classes to become communities of readers – ensuring that they can share in experiences of a wide repertoire of books they enjoy and get to know well.

We support children to become readers by ensuring that they have a balanced and varied diet of key shared reading experiences of which being read to is integral. This is because, as Jim Trelease says in his *Read Aloud Handbook*, when we read aloud to children we are not only entertaining, inspiring, informing and arousing curiosity 'in reading aloud we also:

- build vocabulary
- condition the child's brain to associate reading with pleasure
- create background knowledge
- provide a reading role model
- plant the desire to read'. (Trelease, 2013: 6)

PLANNING A READ ALOUD PROGRAMME

When we plan learning experiences for the pupils in our care, we consider their starting points, their needs and their interests, as well as our aspirations for channelling their curiosity, broadening their horizons and challenging their thinking. These considerations are equally applicable to determining a read aloud programme.

When planning your programme, the first thing you will need to ask yourself is when, how often and how long will you dedicate to reading aloud over the course of the school week?

"HOW OFTEN AND HOW LONG WILL YOU DEDICATE TO READING ALOUD OVER THE COURSE OF THE SCHOOL WEEK?"

Carving out a regular time, place and space for reading aloud will raise the profile of reading, enable you to be a positive reading role model, reap all of the benefits outlined and clearly communicate its value, which will support you in creating a positive reading culture in your classroom. It will be useful to note the following points for consideration when planning your read aloud sessions:

- Who is reading aloud? Consider to what extent children are given the opportunity to experience a range of reading role models. Is there scope to invite special guests such as other members of staff from the site manager, support staff, office staff, Senior Leadership Team to other children? Are there opportunities to engage the wider school community and invite parents and carers into the space?
- Ensure that everyone, both readers and audience, are comfortable. You might choose to have a designated carpeted space with soft furnishings. You may want to sit on the grass outside, under a tree or in a shaded area in the playground, weather permitting. Having a distinctive space that is different from the space in which the everyday learning occurs can add to the special and unique quality of this experience.

- Create a sense that this is an exclusive and special time in the day. You might do this by altering the classroom lighting, switching on some fairy lights, burning a candle or relaxing oils. You could have a decorated story-telling chair or special rug. You might choose to wear a story-telling hat or cloak. You might choose to store the book in a special treasure box or have a playful bookmark. You could have puppets or other props to help you bring the story to life. Such details, however big or small, will help mark the act of reading aloud as an occasion.
- Consider which parts of the day lend themselves best for planned reading aloud and also consider when this is integrated as part of lessons and when this can happen beyond the confines of the classroom.
- Allow for sufficient time to get lost in the moment with the children and make it special – not a hurried, frantic afterthought or add-on.
- Consider the ways in which you might bring the world of the book to life through your tone and expression. Consider how you convey your enthusiasm through facial and physical expressions. Think about how you pace your reading: speeding up to amplify the drama, slowing down to highlight the weight of a scene or incident, and pausing to linger in the moments. Think about ways to invite the children in and join you on your journey through the story.
- Allow for autonomy by creating opportunities for the children to nominate and suggest books that they would like to have read.
- As well as planning carefully chosen books, create a reading basket of delights that can be spontaneously drawn from to shift the energy or for that unanticipated change of plan.

BEING READ TO FROM A RANGE OF BOOKS

When planning your read aloud programme, it is important to ensure that over the course of the term and indeed the academic year children have the opportunity to encounter a breadth and range of genres, writing styles, voices and perspectives. Books that spark a spectrum of core emotions such as laughter, joy, sadness, trepidation, shock and excitement, allowing them to experience fun and adventure as well as explore dilemmas, risk taking and vulnerability within the safe confines of the pages of the text. Books that might be slightly beyond their reading ability, that invite them into worlds that they are not yet ready to venture into independently. Books that serve as affirmations of who they are and offer insights into worlds beyond their own. Books that will challenge and broaden their thinking. By offering a broad and varied diet through your read aloud programme you will make evident the rich and endless possibilities that the gift (Pennac, 2006) of reading affords. You will entice children to want to remain invested in the journey towards becoming confident and competent readers.

EXPERIENCING QUALITY LITERATURE

It is useful to define what constitutes quality literature within this context and determine the kinds of features that should be considered when selecting books for reading aloud.

- Choose books that have the capacity to engage, enthuse, enthral and inspire.
- Select titles that feature memorable, relatable and well-developed characters.
- Source books with dialogue that conveys the relationship dynamics, moves the plot forward and gives you the opportunity to amplify the authenticity, humour, emotion or drama of the scene through your vocal and physical expression.
- Pick books with gripping storylines filled with drama and suspense, so that children hang on your every word and make them bemoan the school bell whenever you're 'forced' to stop reading.
- Share books that are funny and allow you to invite the children to laugh along with you.
- Read books that provoke an opinion, encourage debate, and provide the opportunity to explore dilemmas.
- For children in the early stages of their reading journey select books that will support them in tuning into language, that offer rich models of language, feature repetition, rhythm and strong narrative structures.
- For children in the later stages of their reading journey select books that offer them the opportunity to engage with sophisticated play with language and plotlines, where layered meanings can be pondered upon and inferences and interpretation can be invited.
- Throughout their primary school experience it is important for children to experience books that support and develop their understanding of narrative structures, so that over time they build a bank of reference to inform their understanding of how narrative works.

In terms of text types, it is necessary to ensure that children encounter a good variety of genres and forms to allow them to fully appreciate the vastness of what the world of print has to offer. Sowing the seeds of life-long reading is rooted in sharing classic titles that live long in the memory of children well into adulthood. Such classics should be blended in with emerging contemporary classics.

For younger readers place classroom classics like

- Michael Rosen's *We're Going on a Bear Hunt*
- Trish Cooke's *So Much*
- Julia Donaldson's *The Gruffalo*
- Ezra Jack Keats' *The Snowy Day*
- Maurice Sendak's *Where the Wild Things Are*

alongside budding contemporary classics such as

- Atinuke's *Anna Hibiscus' Song*
- Viv Schwarz's *How to Find Gold*
- Anna McQuinn's *Lulu Loves the Library*
- Joseph Coelho's *If All the World Were ...*
- Tom Percival's *Ruby's Worry*

in the read aloud basket to allow children the opportunity to return to them time and time again.

For older readers share classics like

- David Almond's *Skellig*
- Louis Sachar's *There's a Boy in the Girls' Bathroom*
- Roald Dahl's *Matilda*
- Malorie Blackman's *Pig Heart Boy*
- Phillipa Pearce's *Tom's Midnight Garden*

alongside budding contemporary classics such as

- S.F. Said's *Varjak Paw*
- Catherine Johnson's *Freedom*
- Elizabeth Laird's *Welcome to Nowhere*
- Irfan Master's *A Beautiful Lie*
- A.F. Harold's *Song from Somewhere Else*

Picture books provide an accessible, rich stimulus for engaging a deeply reflective and sophisticated reader response. Powerful books like Emily Hughes' *Wild* for younger children and Armin Greder's *The Island* for older children are prime examples of how illustrations can convey layered and nuanced meanings, inviting the reader to grapple with highly sophisticated and complex themes. Sharing and reading aloud such texts, allowing time to pause and ponder, can create opportunities for meaningful discussion and strengthen the bonds of your reading community.

Traditional tales are moulded for the ear and so commonly feature distinctive patterns and structures to make them engaging and memorable for the audience.

"TRADITIONAL TALES ARE MOULDED FOR THE EAR AND SO COMMONLY FEATURE DISTINCTIVE PATTERNS AND STRUCTURES TO MAKE THEM ENGAGING AND MEMORABLE FOR THE AUDIENCE."

Works by Chitra Soundar, Daniel Morden, Hugh Lupton, Jamila Gavin and Jessica Souhami should grace the shelves of classrooms across the country, and form a core part of the Primary reading diet and the read aloud experience.

Sharing poetry provides children with the opportunity to experience the creative, fun, beautiful and clever ways in which words can be played with to express a thought, feeling or idea. Allowing time to savour the language, ponder the meaning and enjoy the emotions a poem might evoke can make the read aloud sessions poignant, powerful and immensely pleasurable.

Overall, it is important to ensure that children are exposed to a range of text types, genres, settings, places, and authors, written and illustrative styles to ensure a rich breadth of experiences over time. We all have different literary tastes and part of our role as teachers of reading is to give children the opportunity to develop their own thirst and appetite for books related to their interests, humour and personality.

ENGAGING IN SHARED READING EXPERIENCES

By hearing books read aloud, children have the opportunity to experience first-hand what Margaret Meek referred to as the 'rules of the reading game' (Meek, 1991: 111–12).

Reading in our formative stages of development crucially happens aurally. We absorb and internalise the distinctive tunes and patterns of language through the ear. This shapes our early understanding of the purpose of language and how it works (Trelease, 2013).

Hearing words read aloud exposes children to vocabulary that they may be familiar with which helps consolidate their understanding of the varied ways of how and when to use these words, as well as new vocabulary to add to their ever-expanding stock.

The experience of hearing books being read aloud forms the groundwork to support children with their ability to anticipate what to expect when they come to the page, and also equips them to be able to navigate those pages with independence and confidence.

When reading aloud, the reader will give due consideration to the ways in which they express and vary intonation, volume, pitch, dialect, accent and pace. These choices will be informed by the content and an interpretation of the perceived intent of the author. Hearing these choices played out by the reader gives children the opportunity to develop an appreciation for the power of words in the way that they can transport us, form pictures in our mind's eye, generate thoughts and trigger a range of emotions. They will experience the impact of how punctuation and varying sentence length can create a rhythm, alter pace, influence flow or create a sense of urgency. They will encounter the value of structuring sentences and paragraphs in certain ways and ultimately grow to understand the way in which all of these choices shape a writer's style. These important insights will also in time influence and inform children's own writing choices and styles when they themselves come to the page.

REFLECTIONS MOVING FORWARD

- Review your book stock and consider whether you have a sufficient range of quality titles to share with your pupils.
- What core titles will form the basis of your read aloud programme?
- Does the range offer sufficient breadth and range?
- How might you work with the children to determine which books they would enjoy having read aloud?
- How might you begin to build in more opportunities for the children to experience reading aloud?

Time spent planning, reflecting on and evolving your read aloud programme will lay the necessary foundations for a strong, vibrant and positive reading culture in your classroom, and hopefully sow the seeds for a lifelong love of reading.

REFERENCES

Barrs, M. and Thomas, A. (eds) (1991, 1996) *The Reading Book*. London: CLPE.

CLPE (2016) *The Reading Scale*. London: CLPE.

Trelease, J. (2013) *The Read-Aloud Handbook*, 7th Edition. New York: Penguin.

Pennac, D. (Author), Ardizzone, S. (Translator), and Blake, Q. (Illustrator) (2006) *The Rights of the Reader*. London: Walker.

Meek, M. (1991) *On Being Literate*. London: Bodley Head.

CHILDREN'S BOOKS REFERENCED IN THIS CHAPTER

Almond, D. (1998, 2013) *Skellig*. London: Hodder Children's Books.

Atinuke (Author), Lauren Tobia (Illustrator) (2012) *Anna Hibiscus' Song*. London: Walker.

Blackman, M. (1997, 2004) *Pig Heart Boy*. London: Corgi Children's Books.

Coelho, J. (Author) Colpoys, A. (Illustrator) (2018) *If All the World Were ...* London: Frances Lincoln. Books.

Cooke, T. (Author) Oxenbury, H. (Illustrator) (2008) *So Much*. London: Walker.

Dahl, R. (1988, 2016) *Matilda*. London: Puffin.

Donaldson, J. (Author) Sheffler, A. (Illustrator) (1999, 2019) *The Gruffalo*. Basingstoke: Macmillan.

Greder, A. (2008) *The Island*. London: Allen & Unwin Children's Books.

Harrold, A.F. (Author) Pinfold, L. (Illustrator) (2017) *The Song from Somewhere Else*. London: Bloomsbury.

Hughes, E. (2015) *Wild*. London: Flying Eye Books.

Johnson , C. (2018) *Freedom*. London: Scholastic.

Keats, E.J. (Revised Edition 2019) *The Snowy Day*. New York: Puffin.

Laird, E. (2017) *Welcome to Nowhere*. London: Macmillan Children's Books.

Master, I. (2011) *A Beautiful Lie*. London: Bloomsbury.

McQuinn, A. (Author) Beardshaw, R. (Illustrator) (2009) *Lulu Loves the Library*. London: Alanna Max.

Pearce, P. (1958, 2015) *Tom's Midnight Garden*. Oxford: OUP.

Percival, T. (2018) *Ruby's Worry*. London: Bloomsbury.

Rosen, M. (Author) Oxenbury, H. (Illustrator) (1993) *We're Going on a Bear Hunt*. London: Walker.

Sachar, L. (1987, 2016) *There's a Boy in the Girls' Bathroom*. London: Bloomsbury.

Said, S.F. (2003, 2014) *Varjak Paw*. London: Corgi Children's Books.

Sendak, M. (New Edition 2000) *Where the Wild Things Are*. London: Red Fox.

Schwarz, V. (2017) *How to Find Gold*. London: Walker.

CHAPTER 9
DRAMA AND STORYTELLING
DARREN MATTHEWS

The rich and diverse opportunities created by effective classroom drama have meant that it has long been considered by many practitioners as an essential approach in developing children's reading response and comprehension. It invites children to enter into a fictional world, to suspend disbelief, to be creative, to explore characters and their fortunes and misfortunes (either alongside those characters or within those roles), to build empathy and to engage in problem solving. It supports and develops children's ability to comprehend an existing story as well as giving them the space and opportunity to tell their own.

> **"TEACHERS WHO USE DRAMA IN THEIR CLASSROOMS REGULARLY FIND THAT THE VALUE OF THIS APPROACH IS THE IMPACT IT HAS ON YOUNG PEOPLE'S EMOTIONAL AND SOCIAL AWARENESS."**

Teachers who use drama in their classrooms regularly find that the value of this approach is the impact it has on young people's emotional and social awareness – the possibility of stepping into someone else's shoes and exploring the 'what if' of a moment forges a connection between the reader's world and the world of the text leading to an enhanced understanding of both. We learn so much by making comparisons and connections between new knowledge and new skills and what we already know, and by placing us directly in that moment or in that world, drama is a perfectly positioned approach to enhance that learning in a truly accessible way.

When we are selecting and then recreating moments from texts, or when inventing and predicting what we do not yet know from the story, we take all of the explicit and implicit clues the author has provided in the text and combine them with our own personal experiences and understanding of the world to create a virtual embodiment of characters, situation, or setting. This brief moment, this dialogue, or this scene may be one interpretation among many in the classroom, all valid and all valued. In creating and sharing these interpretations children are already involving themselves in an active relationship and dialogue with the text.

Effective classroom drama will inspire rich and deep talk around the text, characters and dilemmas which in turn supports the development of many specific reading strategies and skills: predicting, questioning, visualising, empathising, clarifying, and summarising.

In his book, *Starting Drama Teaching*, Mike Fleming summarises the role of drama in developing and supporting the relationship between text, author and reader: 'Reading and interpretation were seen as essentially passive activities performed on texts with static meanings ... The influence of literary theory, however, has changed the notion of what reading and response in drama entails: "meaning" is more fruitfully seen not as residing in the text according to the intention of the author but as a function of the active meaning-bestowing activity of the reader' (2017: 94).

The impact of drama on children's engagement and progression as both readers and writers are inextricably linked. Teachers who are part of the CLPE Power of Reading programme regularly reflect in both short- and long-term evaluations that the increased use of classroom drama was the teaching approach that made the biggest impact on children's reading and writing engagement: 'Children's focus is shifted from the process of writing to its content. Quite often they forget they are writing! They seem to enjoy writing far more when preceded by drama' (Power of Reading teacher).

Classroom drama provides all participants with a clear voice, purpose and audience, while also supporting composition and content – children are motivated to communicate; they have something to say and a structure within which to say it.

Whether it be stepping into the role of Ivan and setting down the heart-breaking note that you might leave for your parents before you venture out to rescue your brother (inspired by Robert Swindell's *Ice Palace*); or developing our emotional connection to *Blue Penguin* by becoming the whole community of penguins influenced by Petr Horacek's detailed and emotive illustrations; or finding the words to express Frank's torturous experience at the hands of her class bullies in A.F. Harrold's *Song From Somewhere Else*; or creating an entire community that will encounter Kevin Crossley Holland's *Green Children*; children will step away from these safe and inclusive entry points with a deep, lasting and genuine comprehension of the characters' behaviours and choices.

> "A WELL-CONSTRUCTED SEQUENCE OF ACTIVITIES MATCHED AGAINST A WELL-CHOSEN HIGH-QUALITY TEXT WILL BUILD ON AND DEVELOP WHAT THE STUDENTS ALREADY KNOW, ALLOW THEM TO ESTABLISH AND FOLLOW THEIR OWN FASCINATIONS AND CURIOSITIES, AND SHARE AND REFLECT ON THESE WITH EACH OTHER."

A well-constructed sequence of activities matched against a well-chosen high-quality text will build on and develop what the students already know, allow them to establish and follow their own fascinations and curiosities, and share and reflect on these with each other – such an effective approach in developing a community of readers.

> Drama will not teach children the basic skills of reading... Its value in developing reading lies in the exciting contexts it can provide to stimulate higher order skills of inferring meaning from text, of critically engaging with it and, where appropriate, of expressively articulating it. (Winston, 2004: 26)

CLASSROOM DRAMA APPROACHES

The following section summarises some core classroom drama approaches and the potential of each to scaffold and extend children's reading comprehension.

ROLE ON THE WALL

Role on the Wall is a highly effective strategy to support children in discussing, describing and comparing characters, and can be used to explore characters in fiction or non-fiction. Role on the Wall can be planned as a whole class, group or individual exercise, but when the approach is first introduced to a class it does need to be modelled by the class teacher.

To start your Role on the Wall poster, you will need to draw a large outline of the character that is to be explored. This needn't be a literal depiction of the character; a generic 'gingerbread' outline will be sufficient for the task. For a whole-class exercise, you may wish to tape together pieces of sugar paper and then draw around one of the children to produce a sufficiently large version of the silhouette. In the space outside of the outline, write down what the character says and does and their appearance (how they are viewed by others) – in other words the things that are clearly evident from the text or illustration. Within the outline, write down words and phrases to describe their characteristics, their feelings and what they might be thinking on the inside – in other words, we are writing down what we can infer about the character based on their behaviours and appearance. We can give children the opportunity to make explicit links between the external and the internal: how what a character does or say informs us about what they might be thinking or feeling and vice versa.

With some characters, we might return to our Role on the Wall on several occasions throughout our exploration of the text, each time adding a new layer to our understanding. In this instance, using a different colour of pen or pencil each time will allow us to observe the character arc – either how the character changes due to the events that occur, or perhaps how our view of the character changes as new insights are gradually revealed by the storyteller.

At CLPE we have found this to be an effective approach with children of all ages and with all types of text. It works equally well with the Beast in Chris Judge's *The Lonely Beast* or the Monster in Ed Vere's *Bedtime for Monsters* as it does with Ted Hughes' *The Iron Man* or Ted in *The London Eye Mystery* by Siobhan Dowd.

Using Role on the Wall allows the class to reflect in detail about a character. Many reading skills and strategies are authentically utilised during the class's involvement in the activity, including summarising the events and actions from the text, skimming and scanning for pertinent information and behaviours, close reading and clarifying specific vocabulary choices made by the author. When children start from the outside of the outline and move inwards, they are considering what they can infer from a chosen behaviour; when they start from the inside and move outwards, they are looking for the clues in the text that have led them to a particular adjectival phrase.

READERS' THEATRE

Readers' Theatre is an approach that provides children with an opportunity to bring a text to life through performance. It is a highly-inclusive, collaborative activity in which children actively select words, phrases or sections of text to highlight during a short performance, enabling them to engage in discussions around meanings, theme, pattern, rhythm or characterisation.

As with any other activity which is new to a group of children start by modelling the process first: display an appropriate section of the text on the whiteboard or on a flipchart and work together to pick out specific words or phrases and then decide how to perform them and why.

The text chosen for the activity will probably be text that has already been read aloud in class and discussed, so that you are using Readers' Theatre as a mechanism to revisit and examine the language for a closer reading. Select an appropriate length piece of text for the age group that you are working with; something that takes between three and five minutes to read aloud is usually about right. Collectively, the children decide which words, phrases or sentences they wish to emphasise in their performance and mark these on their copy of the text. Next, they need to decide how they are going to highlight these words or phrases in their performance. How are they going to communicate the meaning and the emotional impact through their performance choices? Which words will they read collectively? Which would be more effective read aloud with just one or two voices? Which words might be whispered, sung or shouted? Which might be elongated, slowed down or sped up? Where might an effective pause be held or an echo utilised? How might the punctuation be brought to life in the performance? Would carefully selected sound effects or actions support the group in sharing their vision for the text?

After the group have made their decisions and marked up their copies of the text, they can start to rehearse. During the rehearsal process, they might continue to adapt and refine their choices, until finally they are ready to perform their section of the text. If the same section of text has been used by different groups of children, it will be interesting to compare the different aspects that have been highlighted by their performance choices and why this might have been.

Throughout the Readers' Theatre process, children are actively thinking about language in action – about word meaning, about structure and characterisation, and about effective reader response. We have found it an effective way to help children think about key interaction points in a story, for example when Odysseus meets the Cyclops (*The Adventures of Odysseus*, Hugh Lupton, Daniel Morden and Christina Balit) or when thinking about the language choices such as in *Leon and the Place Between* (Angela McAllister).

FREEZE-FRAME

Freeze-frames are still images or tableaux. They can be used to enable groups of children to examine a key event or situation from a story and decide in detail how it could be represented. When presenting the freeze-frame, one of the group could act as a commentator to talk through what is happening in their version of the scene, or individual characters can be asked to speak their thoughts out loud.

THOUGHT TRACKING

This technique is often used in conjunction with freeze-frame. Individuals are invited to voice their thoughts or feelings aloud using just a few words. This can be done by tapping each person on the shoulder or holding a cardboard 'thought-bubble' above their head. Alternatively, thought tracking can involve other members of the class speaking a chosen character's thoughts aloud for them.

HOT-SEATING

In hot-seating, one member of the class role plays a central character from a poem or story and is interviewed by the other children. This activity involves children closely examining a character's motivation and responses. Before the hot-seating, they need to discuss what it is they want to know and identify questions they want answering. If children have no experience of hot-seating, the teachers may initially need to take the role.

CONSCIENCE ALLEY

Conscience Alley is a useful technique for exploring any kind of dilemma faced by a character, providing an opportunity to analyse a decisive moment in greater detail. The class forms two lines facing each other. One person (the teacher or a participant) takes the role of the protagonist and walks between the lines as each member of the group speaks their advice. It can be organised so that those on one side give opposing advice to those on the other. When the protagonist reaches the end of the alley, they make their decision and communicate it to the rest of the group.

RE-ENACTMENT THROUGH PLAY – ROLE PLAY OR SMALL WORLD

Revisiting stories through a range of play-based experiences helps children to step into the world of the book and explore it more completely.

> **"REVISITING STORIES THROUGH A RANGE OF PLAY-BASED EXPERIENCES HELPS CHILDREN TO STEP INTO THE WORLD OF THE BOOK AND EXPLORE IT MORE COMPLETELY."**

This is important throughout the primary school years and especially with younger children. Opportunities for small world play and role play that are based on a known story promote talk about the shape of the story. They encourage children to discuss key elements such as character and plot and to make decisions about how they create the setting. As they play, whether on their own or in cooperation with others, they practise their narrative skills and 'try on' the different characters using different voices to bring them to life.

Of course, this is just a flavour of the enormous potential for using dramatic approaches to support reader response. All the teaching sequences we produce at CLPE will contain at least one (and usually many more) of these approaches, and there has been a great deal of research and work done in classrooms exploring these approaches for many years. If you would like to read further and more generally about the use of drama in your classroom, a bibliography of suggested and recommended texts is listed at the end of this chapter.

REFERENCES

Barrs, M. and Cork, V. (2002) *The Reader in the Writer* London: CLPE.

Cremin, T. (2015) *Teaching English Creatively*, 2nd Edition. Abingdon: Routledge.

Fleming, M. (2017) *Starting Drama Teaching*, 4th Edition. Abingdon: Routledge.

Prendiville, F. and Toye, N. (2007) *Speaking and Listening Through Drama 7–11*. London: Sage Publications.

Winston, J. (2004) *Drama and English at the Heart of the Curriculum*. Abingdon: Routledge.

CHILDREN'S BOOKS REFERENCED IN THIS CHAPTER

Crossley-Holland, K. and Marks A. (1997) *The Green Children*. Oxford: OUP.

Dowd, S. (2016) *The London Eye Mystery*. London: Puffin.

Harrold, A.F. and Pinfold, L. (2016) *The Song From Somewhere Else*. London: Bloomsbury Children's Books.

Horacek, P. (2015) *Blue Penguin*. London: Walker Books.

Hughes, T. and Carlin, L. (2018) *The Iron Man*. London: Walker Books.

Judge, C. (2011) *The Lonely Beast*. London: Andersen Press.

Lupton, H., Morden D. and Balit C. (2010) *The Adventures of Odysseus*. Cambridge, MA: Barefoot Books.

McAllister A. and Baker-Smith, G. (2009), *Leon and the Place Between*. London: Templar.

Swindells, R. (1992), *Ice Palace*. London: Puffin.

Vere, E. (2011) *Bedtime for Monsters*. London: Puffin.

CHAPTER 10

READING ILLUSTRATION

CHARLOTTE HACKING

Like print, pictures are meaning systems, and it is important that we learn to unravel the meanings that are contained within them. It is equally important that we learn to acknowledge the ways in which these two symbolic meaning systems can work together. (Michaels and Walsh, 1990: 3)

"CHILDREN ARE BOMBARDED WITH A WEALTH OF INFORMATION IN THE CURRENT AGE ... IT IS OUR ROLE AS EDUCATORS TO ENSURE OUR CHILDREN ARE FULLY EQUIPPED TO BECOME WELL-ROUNDED READERS OF THE FUTURE ... "

Children are bombarded with a wealth of information in the current age, with more and more of that information coming to them via the medium of pictures as well as words.

Newspapers, magazines, comics and graphic novels, digital texts, social media, computer games, art, advertising, film and television programmes all require us to use a range of reading skills to interpret meaning from a combination of words and images. It is our role as educators to ensure our children are fully equipped to become well-rounded readers of the future, able to comprehend and analyse fully the messages that may be conveyed in multimodal texts.

> In a world that relies increasingly on visual means of communication, picture books have established themselves as a complex literary genre, in which both verbal and visual cues structure meaning. (Michaels and Walsh, 1990: 3)

Regular planned opportunities for children to read and respond to illustrations in picturebooks are an essential step in preparing them for the complex task of making meaning from text and image, from both visual and verbal cues.

For the last six years at the CLPE, we have been conducting a research project into the use of picturebooks throughout the primary years. We have collected evidence which shows that teaching children how an author/illustrator conveys meaning through words and pictures supports the development of visual and critical literacy skills which are of great benefit to children obtaining a greater depth of understanding as readers and writers.

CLOSE READING OF PICTUREBOOKS

Children are naturally drawn to illustrations in a picturebook and are frequently far more observant than an adult reader. CLPE's research shows that children need time and opportunities to enjoy and respond to the pictures and to talk together about what the illustrations contribute to their understanding of the text.

As teachers of reading we want to help children to appreciate the meanings behind illustrations and to understand and observe devices used by illustrators to convey meaning in the illustrations they have created. But what should we look for when reading? Here are just a few things to begin to investigate when close reading with your children.

FACIAL EXPRESSIONS AND BODY POSITION

Sometimes this can be marked and obvious as in the representation of the cats' initial suspicion and fear of the dog in Viviane Schwarz's *Is There a Dog in This Book?* The cats, whose expressions turn from love to loss and back to love, are drawn with dramatic, very physical reactions which children can easily relate to.

Schwarz, V. (2014) *Is There a Dog in This Book?*, Walker

In some texts, such as Benji Davies' *The Storm Whale*, this is more subtle; the tilt of a head, the twist of a foot or the removal of a mouth can say a huge amount about the personality, emotions or reactions of a character. In selected spreads, Davies chooses to face the character away from us as the reader, inviting us to empathise with the character to comprehend the emotion(s) they may be feeling at this point of the narrative, and enabling us to visualise what this might look like.

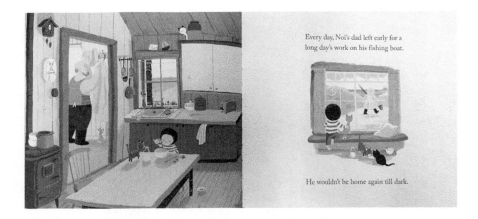

Davies, B. (2013) *The Storm Whale*, Simon and Schuster

PROPS AND VISUAL LINKS

The props that an illustrator draws with their characters increase the reader's understanding about characters. In *Look Up!*, illustrator Dapo Adeola paints a carefully crafted picture of a character through his illustrations of Rocket, the main character. In the initial spread, we are acutely aware of her interest and fascination with space, before this is confirmed in the words on the page. Carefully placed props, like her star earrings, pyjamas, two telescopes, the drawings on her floor, the spacestation toy, the spacesuit carefully lain out on her bed and the fact she has a 'star journal', as well as the patterns chosen for her wallpaper, pyjamas and rug, confirm this is a deep fascination rather than a casual fad.

As we find out more about Rocket and her relationship with her family, scenes in the illustrations give the reader a tenderly observed window into her everyday life. The scene with her mother doing her hair shares how long and intricate a process this is through the placement of two different combs, a brush and two different tubs of product, as well as mum being comfily placed on a soft beanbag – a scene that will resonate with many young readers.

Bryon, N. and Adeola, D. (2019) *Look Up!*, Puffin

In *Grandad's Island* by Benji Davies, we can tell much about the closeness of Grandad and Syd's relationship not only through their symmetry and mirrored body language, but also through the links in the props – Syd's blue striped shopping bag and Grandad's blue striped trousers. Parts of the text and illustration are also linked visually, embedding the voyage and return plot of the story, and highlighting the change in emotion from the light, blue, hopeful togetherness of Grandad and Syd's outward voyage against the grey, choppy return alone by Syd. The spreads of Syd looking up at the attic ladder and of the attic itself at the start of the book are also repeated at the end, but this time without Grandad's legs on the ladder or his most special objects in the attic, emphasising his disappearance.

Davies, B. (2015) *Grandad's Island*, Simon and Schuster

Sometimes, visual links can be used to emphasise a concept in the text. In Laura Carlin's illustrations for Nicola Davies' *The Promise*, we are immersed in the flat, grey city setting right from the front endpapers. Static, linear bricks and fences enhance our perception of the blank uniformity of the setting that physically overpowers the main character in the use of perspective on the title page and first spread. In the first double-spread, the concept from the text that 'No one ever smiled' is enhanced by the placement of the dark black watertowers, central block of flats and the curved bridge, which form a graphic depiction of a sad face.

Davies, N. and Carlin, L. (2013) *The Promise*, Walker

COLOUR

Colour palettes can be specifically chosen for texts. For example, Chris Haughton's books are all defined by their distinct choice of colour from the vibrant orange, red and pink of *Oh No, George!* to the contrast between the cool blues and vibrant greens, pinks and yellows in *Ssh! We Have a Plan*, deepening the sense of trepidation and mystery, allowing the three 'hunters' to camouflage and the object of their interest, the beautifully coloured bird, to stand out against the background, emphasising its intrigue.

At other times colours can be used to symbolise, signify a change of mood or period in time, as is beautifully evidenced in *The Fan Brothers Ocean Meets Sky* where sepia tones are used to represent memories, and the text moves into richer colourful spreads when the main character journeys into a fantasy world of his imagination.

Sometimes colour can be used to reflect mood, as in John Burningham's *Aldo*, where an illustration depicting two adults arguing is washed in red. This technique is also used to great effect by Jon Klassen in *I Want My Hat Back*. The spread where the bear finally realises that his hat has been taken by the rabbit, who has lied to him about seeing it, contains a full-page image of the bear on a red background, facing a page of text which simply states 'I HAVE SEEN MY HAT.'

In *The Promise* by Nicola Davies, illustrator Laura Carlin uses colour to graphically represent the change in both the main character herself, and the change she instigates on the environment as the 'dream' of what could be if she keeps her promise brings the first flashes of bright colour to the text, and as she carries out her promise bursts of colour are seen first in small vignettes and then in two colour double-spreads to emphasise this. Her wider impact on the world as she travels is seen as the colourful vegetation travels with her across the following spreads; first taking up a quarter, then a half, then three quarters of a page before opening up into a full double-spread complete with bright red lanterns. This can also be used to explore the interpretation of this colour in different texts: the red in *Aldo* and *I Want My Hat Back* signifiying anger, and the red here being used to signify prosperity. The flat, uniform grey paving stones in the front endpapers are also transformed in the final endpapers, emphasising the transformation that has occurred throughout the story.

JOURNEY

Lines on the page and directionality of characters can tell us a great deal about how a story progresses or the emotional turns a story may take. One of the most famous examples of this is in Maurice Sendak's *Where The Wild Things Are*, where the pages of the book literally open out as Max's journey progresses until we reach the wordless spreads of the 'wild rumpus'. From the point where Max gets sent to his room, his body faces forward, leading us on to turn the page. He turns back to face the sea creature as he arrives at the place 'where the wild things are', but the boat lurches forward as if to throw him forwards into continuing the journey and the bowsprit of the boat points him forward at each step of the way. In the last scenes of the rumpus, his body turns back, signalling the steps to his return home.

In *Wild* by Emily Hughes, we see the journey of the character played out in the way spreads are used. We are introduced to the main character on a spread where text on the white background on the left-hand side of the spread reads 'No one remembered how she came to the woods, but all knew it was right': the lack of illustration mirrors the lack of memory of these events. Our eye is then drawn to the right-hand side, the direction of reading, to the illustration of the animals caring for the baby, with the accompanying text, 'The whole forest took her as their own'. The illustrations move us through the character's world in the woods where the text tells us 'she understood, and was happy'. Hughes then plays with the directionality on the next page, flipping the illustration to the right-hand side and the text on a white background to the left. This, and the following spreads that all work against the natural direction of the book, help us to understand the interruption in the life of the character. When the main character decides 'Enough was enough', we are led through the right-hand side of the text on her journey back to the forest.

Hughes, E. (2013) *Wild*, Flying Eye Books

FRAMING, LAYOUT AND SEPARATION

In texts such as *Croc and Bird* by Alexis Deacon, pages and spreads are used in different ways for different effects on the reader. The use of frames signals the passing of time and sequential series of steps, as the two main characters hatch from their eggs.

Deacon, A. (2012) *Croc and Bird*, Red Fox Picture Books

The page turn to a larger frame shows their world opening up as Croc goes to search for food, with the guttering in the centre separating him from Bird, deepening the sense of vulnerability around the character.

Vignettes are used to focus on the closeness of the two characters and their relationship, without background elements distracting. Everything revolves around them and their relationship and the rounded edges to the vignettes give a sense of protection, much like the shells of their eggs.

Deacon, A. (2012) *Croc and Bird*, Red Fox Picture Books

In this text, the illustrator chooses when to use a single- or double-page spread, when to convey the story in words and pictures, just pictures or just words. When exploring picturebooks, ask children to talk about the effect each of these things has on the page turn and on our reactions as readers. Spreads where there are pictures but no words force us as the reader to make meaning from what we see, while those that have words but no pictures force us to visualise and empathise.

TIME AND SPACE TO TALK ABOUT ILLUSTRATIONS

It is important to give children time to pore over spreads, looking for and discussing the visual cues that illustrators use to support the reader in constructing meaning and to think about how these work together with the words on the page.

Time spent focusing on reading words and illustration in picturebooks contributes to children's ability to use a wider range of reading skills, read for meaning, express their ideas and respond deeply to the texts they encounter.

> **"TIME SPENT FOCUSING ON READING WORDS AND ILLUSTRATION IN PICTUREBOOKS CONTRIBUTES TO CHILDREN'S ABILITY TO USE A WIDER RANGE OF READING SKILLS."**

Everyone in the class is able to bring their own ideas and prior knowledge to the discussion and this is an important and engaging way of developing critical thinking, vocabulary and the ability to think from different points of view. Mary Roche (2015: 33) shares the importance of this idea in her study *Developing Children's Critical Thinking Through Picturebooks*:

> When a child is listening to a story being read and, when she has the luxury of having time to dwell on the pictures and talk about them, and has time to discuss the book and to co-construct knowledge with peers in a safe and interactive social setting, a whole new sense of making meaning comes into being.

When working with Benji Davies' *Grandad's Island*, one teacher on the Power of Pictures project was able to observe a deeper level of understanding from the pupils in her Year 5 class, watching them notice a far greater level of detail in the illustrations and connecting this to their understanding of characters, and hearing them discuss themes and issues at a far greater depth, drawing on personal knowledge and experiences, than she had previously anticipated:

'We looked at Grandad's Island; what began as a starting activity turned into an in-depth session – mainly looking at the first page, the attic spread and the rich jungle spread towards the end of the text. The children were so excited by their interpretations and were gripped by the story. One of our boys, who barely writes, was able to discuss Grandad at length – the need for his stick as he was becoming vulnerable, the rug in the attic, the suitcases. The final reading was thrilling; one of the children introduced the word 'dementia' which was accurately described with some sadness by many of the children. The vocabulary became richer as time went by, this final reading was electric!'

SUPPORTING THE DEVELOPMENT OF CRITICAL READING SKILLS TO NAVIGATE IN A MULTIMODAL SOCIETY

When we teach children to look at words and pictures in a variety of multimodal texts, we are preparing them to be mindful and critical in a world where digital media, fake news, bias and media manipulation are prevalent.

For example, understanding the underlying structures for conveying meaning in words and pictures is an important strategy for making sense of news in today's society. As Ben Hicks, Executive Director of The Guardian Foundation, reflects in the National Literacy Trust's 'Fake news and critical literacy report' (2018: 20), 'We need to deepen young people's understanding of how the news is produced, learning the processes of interviewing, constructing headlines, choosing pictures'.

Children who are well versed in being able to analyse illustrations and look at the relationships they have with words on the page are far more likely to think critically about how news is portrayed to them by different news outlets.

Many of these concepts and skills will interrelate when discussing art, digital media and film media. You can then extend children's knowledge of specific terminology around these different kinds of media to further deepen their understanding.

THE READER IN THE WRITER: DEVELOPING NARRATIVES THROUGH DRAWING AND WRITING

CLPE's Power of Pictures research project encouraged teachers to work with children on creating their own independent picture-book narratives. A picture-book author must always consider the relationship between words and images so the best way for children to understand this is to create a picture book themselves. The roles of the text and the pictures need to be carefully considered and complementary, not just duplicate one another. When children have spent time deeply reading and responding to picture books this helps them understand how these narratives have been created, the relationships between images and text, and the decisions that have been made by the author and illustrator for impact on the reader.

Working with a variety of authors and illustrators and seeing the ways in which a practising writer works have enabled us to develop a model for writing at CLPE (2018), which shows the significant stages of this authentic process:

Figure 10.1

The process leads them from ideation before they begin to write, through reading, thinking, discussing, drawing and note making before they embark on the creation of a text. Plenty of opportunity is built in for genuine reflection and feedback on the content of the writing before the piece is finally published.

Giving time and space for children to come up with ideas for their own writing before creating texts is an essential part of the writing process – and is linked to their development as readers. You will need to plan for a range of experiences to help children explore and shape their ideas. These could include:

- reading a range of picturebooks, exploring story themes, characters, settings, shapes, structures, patterns and pacing, comparing these to other narratives they have seen or read in film texts, stories and novels;
- engaging in discussions around texts that focus on the impact these make on a reader and identifying techniques that could be used in their own writing;
- time to think, visualise and imagine, through drawing as well as writing;
- engaging in drama, improvising and exploring story ideas, trying out ideas for dialogue;
- exploring and developing ideas through drawing, doodling, note taking and writing;
- discussing ideas with others in a supportive writing community.

Throughout the writing process it is important for children to be given materials and space to allow them to plan and compose ideas in different ways. When children are given opportunities to draw as part of the writing process this helps them to formulate, develop and extend ideas for writing, making their independent self-initiated writing richer. You may wish to give each child a personal sketchbook to develop ideas in and out of taught sessions.

When planning a picturebook, it is important to work out how the story will develop over the given number of pages. Working on small 'thumbnails' allows children to experiment with and work out ideas for how to develop a visual sequence, how spreads will look in a finished book, whether spreads will be single or double page, and how words and images will work together on the page. Children can also plan ideas for book covers, front and end papers, title pages and dedications, allowing them to use and understand the language of picturebook publication in an authentic process.

Harrow Gate Primary, Year 5 Storyboarding

"IT IS IMPORTANT TO DEVELOP CHILDREN AS REFLECTIVE WRITERS BY GIVING AMPLE OPPORTUNITY THROUGHOUT THE WRITING PROCESS TO TALK ABOUT THEMSELVES AS WRITERS, ENABLE THEM TO VOICE THEIR VIEWS, LISTEN TO OTHERS AND DEVELOP NEW KNOWLEDGE AND UNDERSTANDING."

It is important to develop children as reflective writers by giving ample opportunity throughout the writing process to talk about themselves as writers, enable them to voice their views, listen to others and develop new knowledge and understanding. Just as an author would work with an editor, children should be given opportunities to help each other by having their writing read aloud and responding as readers, allowing them to support each other as they compose and structure their ideas. At this stage of the writing, the focus should solely be on content and structure, with responses supporting the writer to get the story they want to the place it needs to be for a reader. Writers can tell response partners what they are pleased with in their writing, or what they may be struggling with. Response partners should reflect on the impact of the narrative and illustrations on them as a reader, asking questions to probe the writer into thinking more carefully about parts of the narrative that aren't working as effectively as they could be. Children can then make additions or re-draft sections of their work, based on these conversations.

At the final stage of the writing process, it is important that children are given time to support each other with transcription proof reading, looking at spelling, punctuation and grammar, and consider the quality of the entire piece before publication. It is also important to give them time and space to work up both the words and illustrations to publication quality, using authentic art materials that match the style the children want to achieve, allowing them to hand write or type and insert text in ways that match their ideas for the overall look and feel of the piece.

St Joseph's Catholics Primary Year 5 Bookmaking

Skills learnt through such writing can then be transferred to the creation of other sorts of multimodal texts, for example, film, news reports for printed or film media or advertisements, leaving children with a much wider and deeper understanding of how words and images can work together to make an impact on readers.

The knowledge and skills needed for this process to be successful can only be achieved if the children have been supported to develop sophisticated levels of inference in illustrations and their relationships with words on the page. As this headteacher from a school on the Power of Pictures project observed:

	Picturebooks to use with children of all ages	Year group specific picture-books	Graphic texts and graphic novels	Comics and magazines	Illustrated novels	Illustrated non-fiction	Illustrated poetry	Film
Early Years	Croc and Bird by Alexis Deacon Shh, We Have a Plan by Chris Haughton	Jabari Jumps by Gaia Cornwall Oh No, George! by Chris Haughton	Stick! by Andy Pritchett	Dot	The Big Alfie and Annie Rose Storybook by Shirley Hughes	Beware of the Crocodile by Martin Jenkins and Satoshi Kitamura	A Great Big Cuddle by Michael Rosen and Chris Riddell	The Penguin Who Couldn't Swim dir. Tom Rourke
Y1/2	Wild by Emily Hughes How to be a Lion by Ed Vere	The Dark by Lemony Snicket and Jon Klassen The Robot and the Bluebird by David Lucas	A Place to Call Home by Alexis Deacon and Viviane Schwarz Traction Man is here by Mini Grey	Storytime Whizz Pop Bang! Okido	Rabbit and Bear: Rabbit's Bad Habits by Julian Gough and Jim Field Claude in the City by Alex T. Smith	Winter Sleep, A Hibernation Story by Sean Taylor, Alex Morss and Cinyee Chiu	Out and About by Shirley Hughes	Baboon on the Moon dir. Christopher Duriez
Y3/4	The Story Machine by Tom McLaughlin Grandad's Island by Benji Davies Is There a Dog in This Book? by Viviane Schwarz	The Promise by Nicola Davies and Laura Carlin Into the Forest by Anthony Browne	Hilda and the Troll by Luke Pearson El Deafo by Cece Bell	First News Anorak National Geographic Kids Scoop The Beano	Oliver and the Seawigs by Philip Reeve and Sarah McIntyre Mouse, Bird, Snake, Wolf by David Almond and Dave McKean	The Bluest of Blues by Fiona Robinson	Things You Find in a Poet's Beard by A.F. Harrold and Chris Riddell	Soar dir. Alyce Tzue
Y5/6	A Mouse Called Julian by Joe Todd-Stanton	The Journey by Francesca Sanna Red in the City by Marie Voight	Roller Girl by Victoria Jamieson Amulet: The Stonekeeper by Kazu Kibuishi	The Week Junior Aquila The Phoenix	The Imaginary by A.F. Harrold and Emily Gravett (Bloomsbury) The Invention of Hugo Cabret by Brian Selznik	Suffragette: The Battle for Equality by David Roberts	Rebound by Kwame Alexander and David Anyabwile	Space Alone dir. Ilias Sounas

"The most surprising thing is that it has given our children a voice and a language. Their developing understanding of how picturebooks work and how illustrators actively make decisions has led to children digging much more deeply into the story. The increasing understanding that the illustrator is an author has led to in-depth discussions around authorial intent. Pupils' increased confidence in expressing understanding and a willingness to challenge ideas has impacted in ways we did not imagine. They have an increasing vocabulary and language to share their ideas."

A well-planned spine of visual texts to include in reading experiences across the primary years, that places an equal emphasis on the visual as well as the verbal in communicating meaning, is an essential consideration for schools to achieve this aim.

REFERENCES

Arizpe, E. and Styles, M. (2016) *Children Reading Picturebooks: Interpreting Visual Texts*, 2nd Edition. Abingdon: Routledge.

CLPE (2019) *The Power of Pictures - Summary of findings from the research on the CLPE Power of Pictures Project 2013-19, June 2019*. https://clpe.org.uk/powerofpictures/research

Doonan, J. (1993) *Looking at Pictures in Picturebooks*. Stroud: Thimble Press.

Michaels, W. and Walsh, M. (1990) *Up & Away: Using Picture Books*. Melbourne: Oxford University Press.

Nodleman, P. (1998) *Words About Pictures: The Narrative Art of Children's Picture Books*. Athens, GA: University of Georgia Press.

Roche, M. (2015) *Developing Children's Critical Thinking through Picturebooks*. Abingdon: Routledge.

National Literacy Trust (2018) Fake news and critical literacy: final report, 2018. London: National Literacy Trust.

FIND OUT MORE

Blake, Q. (2000) *Words and Pictures*. London: Jonathan Cape.

Browne, A. with Browne, J. (2011) *Playing the Shape Game*. London: Doubleday.

Burningham, J. (2009) *Behind the Scenes*. London: Jonathan Cape.

CLPE Power of Pictures https://clpe.org.uk/powerofpictures

Hughes, S. (2002) *A Life Drawing: Recollections of an Illustrator*. London: Bodley Head.

Knight, K. (2014) *The Picture Book Maker: The Art of the Children's Picture Book Writer and Illustrator*. Stoke-on-Trent: Trentham Books.

Lewis, D. (2001) *Reading Contemporary Picturebooks*. Abingdon: Routledge.

Moebius, W. (1990) 'Introduction to Picturebook Codes', in P. Hunt (ed.), *Children's Literature: The Development of Criticism*. Abingdon: Routledge.

Olsen, J.L. (1992) *Envisioning Writing: Toward an Integration of Drawing and Writing*. London: Heinemann Educational.

Oxenbury, H. (2018) *A Life in Illustration*. London: Walker.

Sailsbury, M. (2004) *Illustrating Children's Books: Creating Pictures for Publication*. London: Quarto.

Serafini, F. (2009) 'Understanding Visual Images in Picturebooks', in J. Evans (ed.), *Talking Beyond the Page: Reading and Responding to Picturebooks*. Abingdon: Routledge.

CHILDREN'S LITERATURE REFERENCED IN THIS CHAPTER

Alexander, K. (2018) *Rebound*. London: Andersen Press.

Almond, D. and McKean, D. (illus.) *Mouse, Bird, Snake, Wolf*. London: Walker.

Anorak Magazine, The Anorak Press.

Aquila Magazine, New Leaf Publishing.

Bell, C. (2014) *El Deafo*. New York: Amulet.

Browne, A. (2005) *Into the Forest*. London: Walker.

Bryon, N. and Adeola, D. (2019) *Look Up!* London: Puffin.

Burningham, J. (1991) *Aldo*. London: Red Fox Picture Books.

Cornwall, G. (2018) *Jabari Jumps*. London: Walker.

Davies, B. (2013) *The Storm Whale*. New York: Simon and Schuster.

Davies, B. (2015) *Grandad's Island*. New York: Simon and Schuster.

Davies, N. and Carlin, L. (2013) *The Promise*. London: Walker.

Deacon, A. (2012) *Croc and Bird*. London: Red Fox Picture Books.

Deacon, A. and Schwarz, V. (2012) *A Place to Call Home*. London: Walker.

Dot Magazine, The Anorak Press.

Duriez, C. (dir.) (2003) *Baboon on the Moon*, British Council.

First News newspaper.

Gough, J. and Field, J. (illus.) *Rabbit and Bear: Rabbit's Bad Habits*. London: Hodder.

Grey, M. (2006) *Traction Man is Here*. London: Red Fox.

Harrold, A.F. and Riddell, C (2015) *Things you Find in a Poet's Beard*. Portishead: Burning Eye.

Haughton, C. (2014) *Ssh! We Have a Plan*. London: Walker.

Hughes, E. (2013) *Wild*. London: Flying Eye.

Hughes, S. (1990) *The Big Alfie and Annie Rose Storybook*. London: Red Fox.

Hughes, S. (2015) *Out and About: A First Book of Poems*. London: Walker.

Jamieson, V. (2017) *Rollergirl*. London: Puffin.

Kibuishi, K. (2017) *Amulet: The Stonekeeper* Scholastic.

Klassen, J. (2011) *I Want My Hat Back*. London: Walker.

Lucas, D. (2008) *The Robot and the Bluebird*. London: Andersen.

McLaughlin, T. (2015) *The Story Machine*. London: Bloomsbury.

National Geographic Kids magazine, National Geographic.

Okido Magazine, Doodle Productions.

Pearson, L. (2015) *Hilda and the Troll*. London: Flying Eye.

Pritchett, A. (2013) *Stick!* London: Walker.

Reeve, P. and McIntyre, S. (2013) *Oliver and the Seawigs*. Oxford: Oxford University Press.

Roberts, D. (2018) *Suffragette: The Battle for Equality*. London: Two Hoots.

Robinson, F. (2019) *The Bluest of Blues: Anna Atkins and the First Book of Photographs*. New York: Abrams.

Rosen, M. and Riddell, C. (2015) *A Great Big Cuddle*. London: Walker.

Rourke, T. (dir.) (2018) *The Penguin Who Couldn't Swim*. London: British Council.

Schwarz, V. (2014) *Is There a Dog in This Book?* London: Walker.

Scoop magazine, Curious Publishing.

Selznick, B. (2007) *The Invention of Hugo Cabret*. New York: Scholastic.

Sendak, M. (1963) *Where the Wild Things Are*. London: Red Fox.

Smith, A.T. (2011) *Claude in the City*. London: Hodder.

Snicket, L. and Klassen, J. (illus.) (2014) *The Dark*. London: Orchard.

Storytime Magazine, Luma Works.

Sounas, I. (dir.) *Space Alone* (2009).

Taylor, S., Morss, A. and Chiu, C. (illus.) (2019) *Winter Sleep, A Hibernation Story*. London: Words and Pictures.

The Beano comic, Beano Studios.

The Fan Brothers (2018) *Ocean Meets Sky*. London: Lincoln Children's Books.

The Phoenix comic, David Fickling.

The Week Junior, Dennis Publishing Limited.

Todd-Stanton, J. (2019) *A Mouse Called Julian*. London: Flying Eye.

Tzue, A. (2014) *Soar*, animated short film.

Vere, E. (2018) *How to be a Lion*. London: Puffin.

Whizz Pop Bang! Magazine, Launchpad Publishing.

CHAPTER 11

MODELLING READING AND WRITING

FARRAH SERROUKH

The act of modelling reading and writing allows teachers to deconstruct and demystify the process of reading by demonstrating different parts of the process and offering strategies and approaches to equip children to grow in confidence and competency in this area. It allows children to have the opportunity to develop an appreciation and understanding of what reading is about and by enabling them to join in they also develop a sense of themselves as readers.

WHAT IS THE RESEARCH BEHIND USING THIS TEACHING APPROACH?

Don Holdaway is credited with introducing the practice of shared reading in a systematic way into the infant classroom. In his seminal book, *The Foundations of Literacy*, Holdaway considered how the books parents share with their child, as bedtime stories or favourite books, can become the basis of a child's own playing at reading, their re-enactments of texts and eventually of their learning to read independently. Through his research, he stressed that the regular sharing of certain books was only half the picture; the other half is children's independent practice with familiar texts, and their re-enactments of known stories.

"THE REGULAR SHARING OF CERTAIN BOOKS WAS ONLY HALF THE PICTURE; THE OTHER HALF IS CHILDREN'S INDEPENDENT PRACTICE WITH FAMILIAR TEXTS, AND THEIR RE-ENACTMENTS OF KNOWN STORIES."

He applied this 'developmental model' (Holdaway, 1979: 21–23, 60–63) to the classroom and suggested ways of introducing books – often through shared reading sessions – in which children can join in the reading of books, thereby subsequently equipping them to be able to re-read independently.

Holdaway explored how this approach could be implemented in a methodical way in the infant classroom. He described the stages by which children could move from:

- *discovery* of a new text, in which they get to know the story and begin to participate in the reading,
- to *exploration* of the text, through re-readings and activities related to the book,
- to *independent experience and expression*, when children are encouraged to read or re-enact the text independently or with friends (Holdaway, 1979: 71–72).

Throughout these stages he stressed the ways in which children's attention can be drawn to letter–sound relationships and the structure of words, in the context of the reading.

Holdaway's approach has much in common with Liz Waterland's apprenticeship approach to reading (Waterland, 1985), although he places less emphasis on the teacher reading one-to-one with the child, and more on shared reading experiences with groups and the whole class. Shared reading is the best-known translation into practice of Holdaway's method. The 'three-book approach' (Holdaway, 1979: 65–67) is one in which, during regular reading-aloud sessions, the teacher reads 'one new book, one book that has been heard before and one old favourite'. This is one way that Holdaway suggested would ensure that children have opportunities to re-visit key texts frequently, whilst also being continually introduced to new reading experiences.

"BY MAKING SHARED READING AN INTEGRAL AND ROUTINE FEATURE OF THE PRIMARY EXPERIENCE, TEACHERS ARE ABLE TO PROVIDE A SUPPORTIVE, ENGAGING AND CONSTRUCTIVELY CHALLENGING LEARNING ENVIRONMENT."

By making shared reading an integral and routine feature of the primary experience, teachers are able to provide a supportive, engaging and constructively challenging learning environment.

WHAT PROVISION DO WE NEED TO ENSURE CLASSROOM PRACTICE THAT MODELS READING EFFECTIVELY?

Cultivating a positive, supportive and inclusive learning culture and routines is integral to creating the foundations for nurturing readers. Learning to read is a complex process and one that places great demands on a child's cognitive ability to draw on their prior learning, emotional willingness to take risks and resilience to keep persisting, whilst navigating layers of information to decipher meaning. The classroom practices, teaching approaches and strategies adopted must therefore provide meaningful and effective support to cushion and scaffold a child throughout this process. Modelling in different contexts and in different ways is one of the key means of achieving this.

HOW CAN SHARED READING BE USED TO PROMOTE THE ACT OF READING FOR PLEASURE?

Children will in the first instance need to have experience of sharing books and reading for pleasure and purpose with opportunities to play an increasingly participatory role in reading alongside adults. Sharing books in the early stages of a child's development on the most basic level allows the adult to model how to handle the book as an object. It allows the adult to exemplify which way up to hold the book, how to pore over the details of the page and how to move from page to page, making clear what a child can come to expect from a book both in terms of conventions and experiences. Reading alongside pupils affords adults the opportunity to model enjoyment and the pleasure that can be derived from a book, from laughing out loud to highlight the humour, to gasping with surprise to intensify the drama, to lingering in moments to soak up the emotion.

WHAT ROLE DOES 'TALK' PLAY IN THE SHARED READING PROCESS?

The first and most important resource that young readers need to have is a strong foundation of spoken language. Opportunities must be available for children to develop confidence and competency in their ability to articulate themselves in different contexts; to be able to both express themselves in informal and formal contexts and use talk to help them make sense of their experiences and learning. As children mature as readers, they begin to engage with a greater selection of books and texts. It is crucial that they are supported in their endeavours to take on the multi-faceted reading demands of the curriculum. Children will need to talk about books in order to clarify ideas, relate reading to experience, and reflect on what they have read. This is the real meaning of comprehension. They need to understand that readers respond differently to the same book, and explore the idea that texts or illustrations might be biased, inaccurate or inadequate. If children are well read, they are better able to evaluate what is read and make informed choices. Creating a space and forum for discussion is key to building their understanding in this regard.

HOW CAN I SUPPORT CHILDREN TO ARTICULATE THEIR THINKING?

Allowing opportunities to talk about and respond to what is read and modelling this is key to making explicit the internal dialogue and reflections that arise as we engage with text. We can make this inner dialogue external by thinking out loud and inviting children to engage with us in this endeavour, helping to frame and extend their inner stream of consciousness and initial impressions. This is important in shaping the child's reader identity and developing their understanding of the purpose and complexity of reading, as it makes explicit the validity and value of their thoughts and contributions in constructing meaning and making sense of what has been read. Modelling this one-to-one gives the child the opportunity to vocalise their thoughts and doing the same in group contexts makes explicit that interpretations can be varied and layered.

HOW DO I FACILITATE CONVERSATIONS?

Modelling how to express views with supportive language frames to support children in being able to articulate thoughts and ideas may prove useful. It will be important to invite and value a range of responses and interpretations by facilitating discussions through open-ended and layered questioning to encourage critical reflection, and modelling how to explore lines of enquiry by thinking out loud. Capturing responses by noting thoughts in a group reading journal or working wall will also prove useful in making explicit the ways in which our viewpoint can evolve and change as we travel through a book and that this is perfectly legitimate. These types of modelling make explicit the types of considerations that a reader will experience. The open exploration of such internal processes can go some way towards demystifying the act of reading.

WHY IS IT IMPORTANT TO REVISIT TEXTS AND DEVELOP FAMILIARITY WITH THE CONTENT?

Children at the beginning stages of developing as readers will rely principally on their memory of the story and a willingness to perform, interpret and invent, based on what they have heard and can recall. Readers at this stage may not yet have developed strategies to lift the words from the page. They are familiar with the storyline, the tune on the page, and have a natural inclination to predict when working with memorable texts – so they become the storyteller and re-enact the text. It is this familiarisation that helps these children develop a growing awareness of what is involved in being able to do it themselves. On each occasion and over time, the children will play a more active role in reading. Modelling different ways to revisit, re-enact and re-experience text will be important for consolidating and deepening their understanding and appreciation of the language and narrative structures. You might choose to create story stones, using sharpies to draw key objects relating to a story, or to laminate photocopied characters and attach these to wooden sticks or magnetic strips.

You could have a story sack or story props or puppets to support children in recounting and retelling a familiar story. Draw on these props to model how a story can be recounted, reconstructed, co-constructed and/or retold.

WHAT KINDS OF BOOKS SHOULD I BE USING?

Children need to have knowledge of the conventions of reading, and an understanding of the large (narrative structure) and small (word level) shapes in texts. Children will benefit from experiencing a repertoire of core texts, which broadens over time, allowing for reading material to become increasingly complex and wide-ranging. This should allow for them to be able to respond to texts with increasing inference long before they can decode fluently. A diet of high-quality texts, rich in vocabulary with supportive features with strong shapes and tunes, will enable children to learn how to co-ordinate their use of phonic, semantic and syntactic cues as they become increasingly mature and independent readers.

The text choice for these purposes is key. Drawing on familiar texts provides a supportive framework of reference for meanings and language patterns from which a child can draw, while beginning to focus more closely on print. This allows the adult to make explicit one-to-one correspondence, how to draw on the child's developing phonic knowledge by linking graphemes and phonemes to help them decode simple words and recognition of a core of known words, and how to draw this knowledge together to help them read and understand simple sentences. It is important to ensure the text choice enables an opportunity to practise orchestrating the reading cues, and that we can facilitate growing independence by modelling and supporting children in risk taking and reading aloud by allowing them to re-visit familiar texts and carefully choosing less well-known texts that have supportive features.

HOW DO I ENCOURAGE RISK TAKING WITHOUT COMPROMISING CHILDREN'S SELF-ESTEEM?

One way you might choose to model how to unpick the words on the page with younger children might be by having a puppet that requires support. The puppet shoulders the weight of the task at hand by voicing what they find challenging, which creates a forum to explore with the children what kinds of strategies the puppet might find helpful. This alleviates any anxiety the child or children may have about their own personal challenges, and allows you to model and trial effective strategies and build their resilience without exposing individual inadequacies.

You may choose to invest in different coloured circle stickers, and prior to reading with the children place one colour of sticker under the common sight words that you think they should be able to recall, and a different coloured sticker under the words to which they should be able to apply their decoding skills. When reading with the children you can then pause at each stickered word and model and reiterate how to approach the word. When modelling reading, it will be important to vary your intonation to channel the rhythm and lyricism of the language, as well as highlighting the function of punctuation. Model, in shared and group reading, how to take risks with print by making informed guesses based on semantic, syntactic and grapho-phonic information and using a number of strategies to try out hypotheses, and then confirm or reject these as new knowledge is added to the old. Model and elicit different styles of reading for the demands of different texts encountered, providing experience for a greater variety of books and reading material across all areas of the curriculum.

HOW DO I MAKE EXPLICIT THE INTER-RELATIONSHIP BETWEEN READING AND WRITING?

As mature independent readers pupils will be developing critical awareness as readers, analysing how the language, form and structure are used by a writer to create meanings and effects, and developing an appreciation of how particular techniques and devices achieve the effects they do. They become more able to question and/or admire aspects of content, form and function. Through text marking children can be encouraged to refine their focus, note their observations, and reflect on the impact of choices made by the author.

> "THROUGH TEXT MARKING CHILDREN CAN BE ENCOURAGED TO REFINE THEIR FOCUS, NOTE THEIR OBSERVATIONS AND REFLECT ON THE IMPACT OF CHOICES MADE BY THE AUTHOR."

Modelling this by working with the children to underline, circle, asterisk or colour code words, phrases or sections of text that inspire a response, emotion or thought, gives children the opportunity to consider how honing in on text, re-reading and reflecting can influence and shape understanding.

It would be helpful in the early stages to model directional principles such as finger pointing, return sweep or word location, and you could use a special pointer for this purpose. You might choose to provide some children with word cards that feature common sight words that they will encounter as you read the text aloud and that they are instructed to wave aloft every time these are encountered in the text.

When reinforcing the process of writing into reading, it is important to model writing and reading for a range of purposes across the curriculum. A powerful way to make explicit the interconnectivity of reading and writing and to harness children's learning about what has been read is to empower them to become writers themselves. Through shared writing you can mould the writing process from idea generation to articulation, to language choice to structuring to refinement, culminating in the making and publishing of their own books which can be displayed and re-visited, thus not only giving authorial status to the children but also deepening their understanding of the core transaction between the reader and the writer.

Develop orthographic approaches to reading words and prioritise growing independence in reading and spelling strategies, introducing editing partners, making word collections, and developing self-monitoring and self-help strategies. Make explicit the interdependent nature of reading and writing. Provide rich and meaningful experiences that put the writing system and written language in context, such as bookmaking, using characters, settings, themes or storylines from familiar texts to inspire their own creative writing, writing for a specific purpose and audience. Display such texts as an integral part of the environment in order to develop a sense of authorship.

WHAT OTHER CONSIDERATIONS SHOULD I FACTOR IN WHEN PLANNING AND DELIVERING SHARED READING AND WRITING SESSIONS?

Continue to read aloud regularly, with opportunities for children to participate, question and give opinions. Model reading for purpose and provide meaningful contexts, such as performing poetry, reading for information across the curriculum and collaborative reading opportunities such as 'buddying' areas, in order to increase their confidence in reading to a wider range of audiences. Foster positive reading attitudes and maintain children's confidence in reading by modelling, through shared reading, a wide range of strategies (predicting, sampling, confirming, self-monitoring, and self-correcting), and demonstrating the full range of cueing systems (semantic, syntactic and grapho-phonic).

Encourage improved fluency by supporting children to look at larger chunks of words through a more analytic approach. Provide support by demonstrating rhyme and analogy and using onset and rime to relate unknown words to those they know. Provide word investigations and sorting activities. Intervene sensitively in moving children on, based on close observations in a range of contexts and record keeping. Further embed comprehension and interpretation of texts by developing children's questioning skills and inference. This includes reading illustrations in picture books that may give a deeper meaning than the text on the page. Elicit ideas relating to character motivation, story structure and use of language, encouraging the children to draw on personal experience. Follow up initial responses with prompts that will extend thinking and support reasoning skills.

Demonstrate how to tackle the demands of a range of increasingly challenging reading material through shared and group reading sessions. Reinforce and apply reading strategies in a range of contexts, including exploring specific text features through writing. Scaffold and extend talk through which to express critical thinking, engaging children in debate, discussion and book talk around character, themes and intent.

WHAT PRACTICAL ADVICE WOULD SUPPORT ME IN ORGANISING AND PLANNING HOW TO USE THIS APPROACH?

When planning shared reading it might be useful to keep the following considerations in mind:

Making book choices

1. Do you have a rich and varied range of quality books and wider reading materials that can form the basis of your shared reading sessions?
2. How might you balance the text choices over the course of the term and academic year to ensure opportunities to experience a balanced diet of different text types, literary styles and varied content?

3. Are there opportunities to revisit familiar books as well as encounter new titles?
4. Is your text choice informed by the children's interests and tastes as well as their reading competencies?
5. Do the text choices reflect the realities of your class and school community as well as the wider society?

Timetabling

1. Have you designated routine shared reading sessions on a regular basis?
2. Do children have the opportunity to engage in discussions and reflections about books in different contexts, from one-to-one to small group and whole class contexts?
3. Does the time allotted allow for sufficient scope to meaningfully explore the content and themes of the book?

Planning

1. Have you taken the time to read the book to determine its appropriateness and anticipate the demands of the text?
2. Have you considered marking the stopping points at which to pause for reflection and discussion?
3. Have you planned some open-ended questions to initiate initial responses?
4. What key strategies or approaches do you want to have as the focus of the session?
5. How will you model these in practice? What additional resources might this require?
6. Do you want to engage specific children? Is this better achieved by a one-to-one, group or whole class dynamic?
7. How will you capture the responses?

Evaluation

1. How did the children respond to the book?
2. To what extent were the children able to apply the approaches/strategies?
3. How might you build on the gains made in the session?
4. Have you made a note of each book used so that you will have an ongoing log of all the books explored?

Ensuring the routine practice of shared reading and writing will support you in cultivating a reading and writing culture infused by an enthusiasm for and curiosity and love of language.

REFERENCES

Barrs, M. and Thomas, A. (eds) (1991, 1996) *The Reading Book*. London: CLPE.
CLPE (2016) *The Reading Scale*. London: CLPE.
Holdaway, D. (1979) *The Foundations of Literacy*. Lisarow, NSW: Scholastic.
Waterland, L. (1985) *Read with Me: An Apprenticeship Approach to Reading*. Stroud: Thimble Press.

PART 3

USING HIGH QUALITY LITERATURE ACROSS THE PRIMARY SCHOOL— HOW IT WORKS

CHAPTER 12

DEVELOPING A RICH READING APPROACH IN THE EARLY YEARS

ANJALI PATEL

When developing a rich reading curriculum in the Early Years this needs to be one that makes 'human sense' (Bruce, 2011) to the children. We need to create a rich language and literacy environment that introduces children to the written word in all its forms and demonstrate its potential for expression and communication throughout everyday play provision. It should reflect the cultural, social and linguistic diversity of the children, sending a message that everyone is included, everyone can join the literacy club. Taking time to develop strong relationships with families who can share insights into home lives, languages and literacies, will support us to build on that which is familiar and allow us to introduce the wider world to young children in thoughtful ways.

A well-considered book stock recognises and builds on every child's personal stories, reading experiences, identity, interests and needs.

Quality texts that ignite children's interest in reading can be displayed in enticing ways within the outdoor and indoor reading areas, but they will also be well-placed across the provision to support adults and children to enhance play possibilities or support enquiry. If we interact as interested play partners, spot the potential for literacy development in outdoor play, encourage sustained shared thinking and share quality texts and an irresistible story stimulus, literacy develops rapidly.

Reading is at the heart of the curriculum with provision that shows children it is a valuable and valued activity for everyone in their Early Years community, in which literate acts are constantly demonstrated by more experienced readers and encouraged in the children. Adults who are excited about books are an infectious influence on children's learning. In the Early Years, we are responsible for teaching every child to read. This is one of life's joys but it needs subject knowledge and deserves careful attention. Children don't learn to read because of a twenty-minute focused activity every week. They learn to read all day, every day, and nothing is left to chance by their enabling adults. Reading happens everywhere for purpose and for sheer pleasure.

A high-quality picture book can stimulate exciting and creative learning opportunities. It is wise to keep abreast of the best newly published picture books in order to fully exploit the learning that can be themed around children's interests as well as extend their thinking. And of course, a great book can support our own subject knowledge with concepts we may feel less secure in explaining. Making a wise book choice provides a springboard from which to develop planning that is meaningful, enabling children to explore new ideas in contexts with which they can relate.

Provision rich in rhyme and song, language play and favourite stories from home and school is essential. Read aloud high-quality picture books and other texts daily which will provide exposure to rich examples of writing, illustration and rhythms and patterns of language – stories, poetry, rhyme, information books. Ensure secure book knowledge amongst adults so that they are able to draw on core texts that link to interests, extend play, stimulate talk, and inspire writing. Develop reading routines and texts that evoke possibilities in play, develop thinking, enrich vocabulary, and inspire opportunities to write. Enable children to respond to texts through talk, drawing and role play, and re-visit and re-enact using small world play, puppets or story props. Commit to paper the stories that children tell you, acting as a scribe so that fresh and vivid narratives can reach a wider audience as they are read and enacted by these young authors and their peers.

Providing this foundation of rich reading provision in the Early Years will be a gift for children as they transition to Key Stage 1 and beyond. We want to raise engaged, confident readers who read for pleasure, take an interest in written language in an increasing range of forms, and can access the demands of the curriculum with growing independence.

Reading for pleasure is one of the most significant contributors to lifelong success for our children and is something that can be taught by skilled teachers.

"READING FOR PLEASURE IS ONE OF THE MOST SIGNIFICANT CONTRIBUTORS TO LIFELONG SUCCESS FOR OUR CHILDREN AND IS SOMETHING THAT CAN BE TAUGHT BY SKILLED TEACHERS."

A child who reads for sheer enjoyment benefits from more highly developed communication, language and literacy skills, and the disposition to best access the complex world in which we live. Early Years practitioners can help the children they work with become lifelong readers with all of the benefits this brings. It is worth reflecting then on how we facilitate this with enabling and effective pedagogy, reading routines and text-based teaching approaches.

READING ALOUD

Reading aloud is fundamental to every young child's life and literacy development. It should happen daily as a shared class experience but also when children bring books to us, often the staples, classics and favourites from home such as Julia Donaldson's *The Gruffalo*, Martin Waddell and Patrick Benson's *Owl Babies*, Maurice Sendak's *Where the Wild Things Are*, or Judith Kerr's *The Tiger that Came to Tea*. Shared experience, preferences and enjoyment as a class support children's transitions from home or pre-school, their sense of security and well-being, and their identity as an individual reader and as a class community. Listen out for books that read aloud well and model the art of reading aloud for less experienced or confident adults.

Choose books that allow children to enter the fictional world of a story which feature human themes and characters with whom children can make personal connections. These might be stories that play out childhood concerns in familiar scenarios such as those in Shirley Hughes' *Alfie Stories* or *Jabari Jumps* by Gaia Cornwall, or they could involve less familiar settings and, of course, object or animal protagonists, such as *Brave Bear* by Emily Hughes or *Naughty Bus* by Jan and Jerry Oke. Take care to provide a balance so that all your children are able to see their realities reflected in these stories and the scenarios and characters they portray.

Place poetry, rhyme and song at the heart of your read-aloud programme by linking daily experiences of singing with your book stock of nursery rhyme collections and printed versions of songs such as those published by Child's Play. Hearing and joining in with the Ahlberg's *Each Peach Pear Plum* will be a gift that will last a child a lifetime. Poetry collections like *Here's a Little Poem*, collected by Jane Yolen and Peter Fusek Peters, and *A Great Big Cuddle* by Michael Rosen and Chris Riddell will broaden the children's range of reading experience and provide comforting and amusing themes for children to draw on.

Books with patterned language which inspire children to chime in bring a sense of participatory enjoyment to the read aloud and with the fun will come some serious teaching opportunities. Children will be developing an ear for language and increasing their repertoire of rhyming words to support predictions, using prosody to aid memorisation. They will soon learn by heart the rhythmic refrains of books like *The Night Pirates* by Peter Harris and then use this knowledge to read along with you, thus linking what they have heard and said to the words they see on the page. They will absorb the tunes of written language and become sensitised to the written word through the act of storytelling. In effect, they are being exposed to literary structure, drawing on knowledge of the 'big shapes' to aid prediction and fluency. Read aloud and tell plenty of traditional tales with strong narrative structures, thereby supporting a class culture of oral storytelling.

"READ ALOUD AND TELL PLENTY OF TRADITIONAL TALES WITH STRONG NARRATIVE STRUCTURES, THEREBY SUPPORTING A CLASS CULTURE OF ORAL STORYTELLING."

Once they have learned the basic structure of stories like *Little Red Riding Hood*, children will enjoy hearing versions of the tale read aloud, exploring the variations and discussing which most appeal to them and why.

Very young children will often write for expressive purposes, sharing their disgruntlement that they miss mummy at drop-off or communicating personal information about their family. As they settle into the classroom culture their experiences will broaden, and they will begin to engage in sharing information with peers and in response to books in the form of labels, lists, captions and messages. Reading aloud non-fiction texts related to their interests and fascinations will help children tune into their voice. Writing opportunities in the garden area could be supported by hearing *Yucky Worms* by Vivien French read aloud, or perhaps reading craft books like *Make with Maisy* by Lucy Cousins could inspire new ideas in the creative area, as well as providing children with models for creating their own instruction booklets.

Choose a book with illustrations of artistic merit that support the retelling as well as providing an opportunity for a deeper exploration of aspects of the story, such as character behaviour, feelings or events. Do the pictures encourage conversations with the potential for talk and discussion on a number of levels? Do the illustrations tell a story other than or in addition to the text, such as in the seminal *Rosie's Walk* by Pat Hutchins or the more contemporary *Shh We Have a Plan* by Chris Haughton. Often these books will provide humorous storyline in which children will collude with the illustrator whilst an 'unsuspecting' adult reads the text aloud.

WORKING WITH A BOOK IN MORE DEPTH: *BEDTIME FOR MONSTERS* BY ED VERE (PUFFIN)

CREATING A STORY CHARACTER

- Make some 'Monster Footprints' to leave out in the classroom on the morning that the book study will begin.
- Have the children walk in to find the footprints. Who do we think they belong to? Scribe children's ideas in speech bubbles as a record of the talk. Without sharing the front cover of the book, look at the footprints and text on the first pages and read aloud.

Allow children time to look and respond to the question asked in the text: 'Do you wonder if somewhere, not too far away, there might be MONSTERS?'. Scribe ideas in the shared journal around a copy of the picture of the monsters.

- Look at the illustration of the monsters. Are they all the same or are they different? Talk about the different monsters in the picture, making notes of good examples of descriptive vocabulary.

- Make provision for children to create models of their own monster using play dough, junk modelling and embellishments or drawing. Crucially, as they are immersed in their creations, the children are internally developing vocabulary which can be further extended through talk.

- Children can tell a friend about them and introduce them to each other's monsters. Create recipes together to feed the monsters and routines to care for them.

- Encourage the children to explore and play with their monsters, finding out what they could do with them. Give children time to create small world settings, stories and dialogue involving their monsters. Allow lots of opportunities for drawing and mark making on a large scale. Rolls of paper indoors or out give good scope for shared illustration on a large scale, or children could respond by painting or smaller scale illustration using a variety of media or a digital graphics program. These could be put together with children's speech into a shared 'Our Monster Adventures' book.

- Send a toy monster home to spend the weekend with a child from the class. Make a special monster-shaped book to accompany this and encourage children to record the adventures they have together in any way they like, using a combination of photographs, drawings, writing or annotation.

- Encourage parents to also join in, perhaps adding comments or scribing the story for their child. On the monster's return to school, children should share the weekend's events with the class, using the book to help them talk about what they did together.

- Read to 'You're not scared are you?'. Discuss this question and talk about the different responses. Texts should be a secure world from which to explore and talk about fears in a non-threatening way.

- What could we do if we're scared of the monster? Investigate ways of keeping him out such as making a 'Keep out!' sign, labelling bottles of monster spray, writing up emergency plans, or designing, constructing and labelling a monster trap.

LOOKING AT LANGUAGE AND READERS' THEATRE

- Re-read and re-enact the monster's journey through play. Look at the illustrations carefully. How does the author/illustrator describe the setting in words and pictures; can you picture what it is like to be there?

- Ask the children to share the words and phrase that they find most memorable or vivid. Model how to scan an enlarged version of the text for these words and highlight them. Why have they chosen these? How do they sound? How do they feel when you articulate them? Explore the aural and visual patterns that grab the children's interest in the pairing of words like gloopy/schloopy, scritch/scratch, squished/squashed, thorns/thistles.

- Sensory experiences can be provided in small world play to explore the settings of the wood, swamp, thorns and thistles, and mountains. And if possible, take a trip to a local park or wood to discover first-hand the outdoor elements of the setting. Allow children to explore 'schlooping' with wellies through thick, gloopy mud, or climb up steep inclines to understand the struggle experienced by the monster, or watch a snow blizzard scene on film and use paint to depict it – all the time revisiting and modelling children's use of descriptive language from the book.

STORY MAPPING AND SHARED WRITING

- Focus on the illustrations of the monster throughout the story, without the text. Collect children's words to describe the monster, encouraging them to look closely at what they can see in the pictures. What does he look like? What does he do?
- Read aloud the book several times, encouraging the children to join in with the repetitive refrain, and become familiar with the strong story shapes and structure in their own retelling.
- Focus on children recalling and using descriptive language from the text to describe the different settings in the journey and how he travelled. Recap on the main events in the story and swiftly map out the story on a long roll of paper using images and some key phrases.
- Together, retell the story orally, evoking the mood or atmosphere of favourite scenes through intonation, vocal expression or even instrumental sound effects. Children might create a soundscape of the whole story, using the story map as a guide to denote sequences of events, setting changes, and shifts in mood or atmosphere.
- Children can then take their salt dough, crafted or puppet monsters on an adventure from their box home and around the setting, taking photographs or making their own story map of where their monster has been. This could also be done at a place of interest outside the setting to vary the places the monster travels to on his journey. The children might be inspired to research a range of geographical settings in which their monster could inhabit and use postcards or images from books as a fitting backdrop.
- Take some of the photographs or illustrations of the monster journeys on the IWB. Choose one to focus on. Can the children see where the monster was or what he was doing? Discuss and explain that you want to write some captions for the photographs so that you can put them on display in the classroom. Explain that a caption describes what is happening in the photograph.

TEACHING EARLY READING SKILLS AND STRATEGIES

DEVELOP PHONOLOGICAL AWARENESS – ALLITERATION: *STANLEY'S STICK* BY JOHN HEGLEY AND NEAL LAYTON

- Read aloud *Stanley's Stick*.
- Re-read the first page of the story to the children. Enlarge the page so that the children can see the print: 'Stanley stands on Stockport Station with his stick.'

- Ask the children to listen carefully and talk about what they can hear. Can they hear the alliteration? Have a bag of objects and ask the children to pass the bag around and look inside. Can the children name the objects in the bag? (Include objects such as a stick, stone, string.)
- Invite children to think of any other words that begin with 'st'. Do any of the children's names have this sound in them? Make a word collection on a large piece of paper for the children to add to independently if they find or can think of any more 'st'words. Can they hear the rhyme/alliteration?
- You might swap the objects in the bag to include object pairs that rhyme or that have the same sound at the beginning other than 'st' (spoon/moon, goat/coat, stick/stone).
- Invite children to think of any other words that rhyme or begin with the same sound. Do any of the children's names have this sound in them?

DRAW ATTENTION TO PRINT THROUGH FAMILIAR RHYMES AND SONGS

- Choose books for this with strong tunes and patterned language and that enable demonstration and practice in orchestrating reading cues and strategies.
- Sing a favourite nursery rhyme like 'Hickory Dickory Dock' as a group.
- Provide pairs of children with an attractive illustrated rhyme card so that they can tune into the printed words and phrases that they are so familiar with, making explicit directionality and one-to-one correspondence.
- If children have phonic knowledge, draw attention to a known grapheme–phoneme correspondence such as /ck/ and support them to apply their blending skills by synthesising phonemes through a word.
- Explore rhyming pairs that the children hear and draw attention to their visual spelling pattern. Make collections of single-syllable rhyming words with the same onset and rime pattern, such as dock, clock, rock, to help develop fluency.
- You could build a class collection of core stories, songs and rhymes (commercially produced or home-made) that the children can listen to and then practise matching the spoken to the printed word in familiar contexts. Create a core collection of rhymes and songs and share this with the parents, sending home song and rhyme sheets for the children to learn and tune into the printed words on the cards.
- Find books like *Hickory Dickory Dog* by Alison Murray that mirror the rhythm of known nursery rhymes and play with the lyrics to tell a new story. What strategies can the children use to read this version?
- Find quality texts like *Hop on Pop* by Dr Seuss, *The Cat Sat on the Mat* by Brian Wildsmith or *Shark in the Park* by Nick Sharrett that enable children to practise and apply decoding strategies in stimulating contexts.

BOOK-BASED GAMES TO SUPPORT EARLY READING

- In book-based reading games, familiar phrases from books that children know well can be used as part of the games. Familiarity is essential in developing early reading strategies and re-reading text interactively in this way reinforces the permanent nature of written print. Books involving journeys or strong connections between illustrations and text like *Hurray for Fish* by Lucy Cousins are ideal.

- You could create a track game, acknowledging the journey of the story and incorporating the physical locations visited. It should include opportunities for the children to read familiar words and phrases from the text and signs in the illustrations, and then link movement along the track with events in the narrative.
- Alternatively, you could make a pairs game to develop visual memory and book language, creating cards using laminated images from the book. Make two sets of picture cards for the characters, places and key features of the story. Spread these out face down on the table/floor. Children then take turns to turn over two cards. If they are the same they can keep them, if not they have to turn them back over again. The game proceeds until all the pairs have been found.

SUPPORTING INDEPENDENT READING

- The beginner reader has to learn to bring together different kinds of knowledge and draw on the different kinds of cues available to them in the texts you choose. Some children may prefer to maintain pace and flow in their reading and attend to the overall meaning of the text; others will favour accuracy, focusing their attention on each word at a time; most will achieve a greater balance in their reading with time and experience. If we want to develop independence, we need to find the books that engage each child's favoured style of reading whilst also enabling them to practise orchestrating a wider range of skills and strategies. We need to ease the process of reading and support their inner drive to find meaning from the print even without the support of an adult.
- It is crucial at these tentative stages that we help shape reader identity in our youngest children. They need to see themselves as readers and to engage in reader-like behaviours. This is where collections such as the CLPE's *Core Books, Learning to Read* collection can support you to have a selection of books that will ensure you are providing independent materials that will facilitate the children to apply their growing reading skills and strategies, but that will also enable them to explore rich texts and develop their comprehension and inference skills at the same time. Children need to be provided the time opportunity to explore rich book stock for themselves and to read freely as well as when directed by adults.
- Once the children have memorised the language of a story through repeated readings, they can be given copies of the story to read to partners. This helps children to see themselves as readers. They can be supported in tuning into the print on the pages, applying their understanding of one-to-one correspondence to familiar words and phrases.
- Source or create audio books to which children can listen to a familiar story read aloud whilst tracking the print on the page, taking a signal to page turn. As well as stories, make accessible favourite songs in published form, such as 'The Animal Boogie' by Debbie Harter.
- Choose books that provide an opportunity to explore learning across all areas of learning and can be re-read and re-visited in a range of contexts and through play provision, like

Counting with Tiny Cat by Viviane Schwarz, *Roadwork (Construction Crew)* by Sally Sutton and Brian Lovelock, or *A Tiny Seed* by Eric Carle.

- Make explicit in your phonics teaching how children can apply their increasing knowledge of grapheme–phoneme correspondences to reading real, high-quality picture books; not only books with immediately recognisable decodable elements but also those that allow them to draw on other cues and knowledge.
- Encourage an ethos of peer recommendation and making links with parents, bookshops and libraries that can further the children's engagement in books will make all the difference in sustaining children's motivation beyond their acquisition of the basic skills of reading. But ultimately, knowing your young readers and being a reading teacher yourself will support you to make the best recommendations that are best suited to each individual.

REFERENCES

Barrs, M. and Cork, V. (2002) *The Reader in the Writer*. London: CLPE.

Bromley, H. and Barrs, M. *Book Based Reading Games*. London: CLPE.

Bruce, T. and Spratt, J. (2011) *Essentials of Literacy 0-7: A Whole-Child Approach to Communication, Language and Literacy*. London: Sage.

CLPE (2016) *The Reading Scale*. London: CLPE. https://clpe.org.uk/library-and-resources/reading-and-writing-scales

Chambers, A. (2010) *Tell Me Children (Reading and Talk) and The Reading Environment (How Adults Help Children Enjoy Books)*. Stroud: Thimble Press.

Holdaway, D. (1979) *Foundations of Literacy*. Lisarow, NSW: Scholastic.

Mallett, M. (2003) *Early Years Non-Fiction: A Guide to Helping Young Researchers Use and Enjoy Information Texts*. Abingdon: Routledge.

Meek, M. (1987) *How Texts Teach What Readers Learn*. Stroud: Thimble Press.

Nutbrown, C. (2011) *Threads of Thinking*. London: Sage.

Palmer, S. and Bayley, R. (2005) *Early Literacy Fundamentals: A Balanced Approach to Language, Listening, and Literacy Skills*. Arkham, ON: Pembroke.

FIND OUT MORE

A comprehensive selection of high-quality books for children from ages three to eleven https://clpe.org.uk/corebooks

Choosing and Using Quality Children's Texts: What We Know Works https://clpe.org.uk/library-and-resources/what-we-know-works-booklets/choosing-and-using-quality-childrens-texts-what-we

The Power of Reading: Building a Text-based English Curriculum https://clpe.org.uk/powerofreading

CHILDREN'S BOOKS REFERENCED IN THIS CHAPTER

Ahlberg, A. and Ahlberg, J. (1999) *Each Peach Pear Plum*. London: Puffin.

Carle, E. (1997) *A Tiny Seed*. London: Puffin.

Cornwall, G. (2018) *Jabari Jumps*. London: Walker.

Cousins, L. (2013) *Hurray for Fish*. London: Walker.

Cousins, L. (2002) *Make with Maisy*. London: Walker.

Donaldson, J. and Sheffler, A. (2017) *The Gruffalo*. Basingstoke: Macmillan.

Dr Seuss (2017) *Hop on Pop*. New York: HarperCollins Children's Books.

French, V. and Ahlberg, J. (2015) *Yucky Worms*. London: Walker.

Harris, P. and Allwright, D. (2007) *The Night Pirates*. London: Egmont.

Harter, D. (2011) *The Animal Boogie*. London: Barefoot Books.

Haughton, C. (2015) *Shh We Have a Plan*. London: Walker.

Hegley, J. and Layton, N. (2013) *Stanley's Stick*. London: Hodder Children's Books.

Huchins, P. (2009) *Rosie's Walk*. London: Red Fox Picture Books.

Hughes, S. (1990) *The Big Alfie and Annie Rose Storybook*. London: Red Fox.

Kerr, J. (2015) *The Tiger that Came to Tea*. New York: HarperCollins Children's Books.

Murray, A. (2012) *Hickory Dickory Dog*. London: Orchard Books.

Oke, J. and Oke, J. (2005) *Naughty Bus*. Little Knowall Publishing.

Rosen, M. and Riddell, C. (2015) *A Great Big Cuddle*. London: Walker.

Schwarz, V. (2019) *Counting with Tiny Cat*. London: Walker.

Sendak, M. (2000) *Where the Wild Things Are*. London: Red Fox.

Sharrett, N. (2017) *Shark in the Park*. London: Corgi Children's Books.

Sutton, S. and Lovelock, B. (2011) *Roadwork (Construction Crew)*. Somerville, MA: Candlewick Press.

Taylor, S. and Hughes, E. (2017) *Brave Bear*. London: Walker.

Vere, E. (2011) *Bedtime for Monsters*. London: Puffin.

Waddell, M. and Benson, P. (1994) *Owl Babies*. London: Walker.

Wildsmith, B. (1982) *The Cat Sat on the Mat*. Oxford: OUP.

Yolen, J. and Fusek Peters, A. (eds) Illustrated by Dunbar, P. (2010) *Here's a Little Poem*. London: Walker.

CHAPTER 13

DEVELOPING A RICH READING APPROACH IN KEY STAGE 1

KATIE MYLES

Young children moving from the Early Years Foundation Stage into Key Stage 1 are at an important moment in their reading journey, as these developing readers are beginning to gain control of the reading process and with the right support will be well launched on reading by the time they leave Key Stage 1. Having moved from their dependence on memorisation and reading alongside an adult, the majority of children will now be ready to begin to explore new types of texts on their own and will develop fluency with the right input.

Learning to read however is a complex process and one that places great demands on a child's cognitive ability to draw on their prior learning and emotional willingness to take visible risks.

"LEARNING TO READ HOWEVER IS A COMPLEX PROCESS AND ONE THAT PLACES GREAT DEMANDS ON A CHILD'S COGNITIVE ABILITY TO DRAW ON THEIR PRIOR LEARNING AND EMOTIONAL WILLINGNESS TO TAKE VISIBLE RISKS."

This is especially at a time of great change as the children move from their early year settings, characterised by play and exploration, to more formal classrooms. Children will therefore need to have continued and sustained experiences of reading for pleasure and purpose and opportunities to engage in reading behaviours across the curriculum.

Children in Key Stage 1 will need to have knowledge of the conventions of reading, and an understanding of both the large and small shapes in texts. A diet of high-quality texts, rich in vocabulary with supportive features and strong shapes and tunes, will therefore enable children to learn how to co-ordinate the use of phonic, semantic and syntactic cues as they become increasingly fluent readers. They will also continue to benefit from a repertoire of core texts and be able to return to firm favourites as well as being introduced to new texts that will broaden their reading experiences, especially as they will be able to respond to complex texts with increasing inference long before they can decode fluently.

The rich reading curriculum on offer will incorporate a range of reading experiences to support the children's reading development. These can be characterised as 'reading *to* the children, reading *with* the children and reading *by* the children' (Elborn, 2015: 8). Our provision will therefore include a planned read-aloud programme, shared and group reading, one-to-one reading, time for independent reading, and a systematic, synthetic phonics programme.

READING ALOUD

Reading aloud needs to be a frequent and regular part of each school day. This is in part because reading aloud slows written language down and enables children to hear and take in tunes and patterns. They are also able to hear fluent and expressive reading modelled by a mature and independent reader. This enables children to experience and enjoy stories that they might not otherwise come across.

Before reading a book to a class, it is always important for teachers to read it themselves as reading aloud is a kind of performance. It's therefore helpful to think about the best way to read it and 'lift it off the page' in order to engage children and enable them to respond to both the tunes and the meaning. By reading well-chosen books aloud teachers also help classes to become communities of readers, ensuring that they can share in experiences of a wide repertoire of books they will enjoy and get to know well.

To support the transition from Reception, it is advisable to begin the new academic year reading aloud and revisiting a range of favourite picture books, poems and rhymes, before introducing new texts.

Building on the types of stories children are already familiar with, the modern classic *A Dark, Dark Tale* by Ruth Brown allows children to continue to tune into repetitive language, to enjoy pattern and rhyme, and to further internalise the ways in which narratives 'work'. They thoroughly enjoy the surprise twist at the end of this book which shows how repetition can build excitement. The combination of a very simple written text with sombre and enticing illustrations also casts a mysterious spell and gives a wide range of readers access to the book.

Traditional tales have a central role within a KS1 rich reading curriculum, and work very well as books to read aloud as they are stories which were originally moulded for the ear. Traditional tales contain considerable repetition, rhythm and sometimes rhyme, which make them easy for children to chime in with and recall. In *Pattan's Pumpkin*, storyteller Chitra Soundar has adapted a flood story from one told in Kerala in southern India. Pattan and his wife Kanni grow food which they share with all living creatures. An ailing plant that he nurtures becomes a huge and splendid pumpkin, which provides rescue and shelter when dark clouds gather and a flood threatens the human, animal and plant life.

This book allows children to begin to make inter-textual connections as they draw comparisons with other stories they have read, such as *The Gigantic Turnip, Mr Wolf and the Enormous Turnip* and *Pumpkin Soup* as well as flood stories such as *Noah's Ark*. The text also offers young readers a good stimulus for their own descriptive and story writing as well as providing the chance to learn about the Indian Subcontinent and the animals that live there if they so wish. The children would also be able to draw on the strong language structures which lend themselves well to structuring oral and traditional storytelling.

"FINDING TIME TO 'TELL' STORIES TO YOUR CLASS AS PART OF THE STORYTIME SESSIONS WILL ALSO OFFER OPPORTUNITIES FOR CHILDREN TO DEVELOP AS STORYTELLERS THEMSELVES, THEN OVER TIME THEY WILL LEARN TO EMPLOY STRONG NARRATIVE STRUCTURES AND USE RICH AND MEMORABLE LANGUAGE IN THEIR OWN FICTIONAL NARRATIVES."

Wherever possible, finding time to 'tell' stories to your class as part of the storytime sessions will also offer opportunities for children to develop as storytellers themselves, then over time they will also employ strong narrative structures and use rich and memorable language in their own fictional narratives.

A collection of short stories such as *Anna Hibiscus* by Atinuke would work well as a read aloud as your young readers continue on their reading journeys throughout Key Stage 1, as it will support building reading stamina. It will also help children to access material beyond their instructional level and will support language and vocabulary acquisition, as well as supporting their developing knowledge of more complex grammatical structures.

These separate but connected stories are about the life of a small girl who lives in Africa with her African dad and Canadian mum and a large extended family. Modern and traditional aspects of African life are an integral part of the stories. Texts like this are therefore also important as they are representative of personal experience and a range of cultures and traditions. This will help children to make text-to-self connections which support reading comprehension, as well as fostering an enjoyment of reading.

The books you read aloud will also be the types of book that children will want to re-read with peers or on their own, so it is important to place these in the class book corner or somewhere accessible so that children can take the opportunity to engage more deeply with these after you have read them aloud on multiple occasions. This will particularly support less experienced readers or those for whom English is an additional language, as re-reading helps to make the text more familiar and enables children to read it more confidently, fluently, and with greater attention to the meaning.

BOOKS TO WORK WITH IN MORE DEPTH

A rich reading diet will include a range of texts, some of which will be enjoyed when read together but that do not offer wider opportunities for learning. For a book to be suitable as a class text, around which teachers and children can develop discussion, writing and creative work, it therefore needs to be worth revisiting. It should inspire thinking and creativity, provoke questions, and lead to learning opportunities across the curriculum. The text should also allow you to deepen the children's responses and encourage them to make connections by exploring other texts by the same author or on the same theme.

RAPUNZEL BY BETHAN WOOLLVIN

This pared back and twisted take on a traditional tale, told with the humour to be gleaned from reading the pictures, works perfectly as a whole-class text. It begins with Rapunzel, portrayed as a child, already encased in the tower without the back story explaining how she came to be there, and reaches a conclusion in which she makes a joyful escape *without* the aid of a prince:

- The book allows you to explore characterisation and particularly characters that defy convention or expectation. As the text is simple, close reading of the illustrations enables the children to find out more about the way in which the author/illustrator has communicated ideas about Rapunzel's character and personality. Using an approach such as 'Role on the Wall' is a useful way of supporting children to understand characterisation, and especially how an author or illustrator often 'shows, not tells' a reader.
- The approach uses a displayed outline of the character to record feelings or inferences (inside the outline) and outward appearances or facts and information (outside the outline) at various stopping points across the story. Using a different colour at each of the stopping points within a text allows you to track changes in the character's emotional journey or a reader's perceptions of a character.
- With this particular text you can ask the children to consider Rapunzel's character early on in the story, when it may appear that this tale is a simple re-telling of the original, and again later on in the text when they have realised that she is very modern heroine who can save herself. The children may also bring prior knowledge of the story to the text, and as the story unfolds it will be interesting to see how their initial perceptions of the character Rapunzel alter.
- Reflect on the twist in the story from the original version; the fact that Rapunzel isn't frightened of the witch and that she was able to use her intellect to leave the tower the same way the witch got inside, as well as the absence of a male 'hero'. You could therefore return to the Role on the Wall and ask what her escape suggests about Rapunzel and her personality, considering if the children's initial perceptions of her personality and character have changed. Scribing the children's responses in a different colour would highlight any changes in opinion they may have of her character.
- To consolidate understanding and the appropriateness of the language chosen, you could build on this using the 'zone of relevance' approach (https://clpe.org.uk/powerofreading/teaching-approaches).
- Place the children into small groups, and give each group a target template. Then give the them a range of vocabulary that could describe Rapunzel and her personality but also some 'red herrings' which are not relevant.
- Ask the children to discuss the selection of words to describe Rapunzel and then to sort them onto the diagram, with you, or another adult, clarifying meaning where necessary.

If a word is irrelevant, the children can place it outside the target. If it is relevant, they have to decide how relevant and the more relevant it is, the closer it must be to the centre of the target. Collecting and exploring words in this way will support children to have a more focused awareness of the ways language affects our perceptions and understandings, and the ways in which the author creates the readers' response. They can then add these words to their own developing vocabulary and will be more able to go on to use them in their own writing.

- This deeper exploration of both text and character naturally leads to the children wanting to inhabit the characters and engage in role play and drama. Returning to the moment in which Rapunzel leaves the tower, the children will want to consider how it must feel to be Rapunzel in this moment, her first time outside of the tower. To support this, you may want to take them outside and ask them to imagine it is the first time they have ever felt the grass, seen the trees up close, the birds and the insects. At this moment you could ask the children to tell you what they notice about the sights, sounds, colours, shapes, sensations and smells they notice that they think Rapunzel would have been excited by.

- Using an approach such as freeze frame and thought tracking will support the children in understanding how Rapunzel feels at this point, as will encouraging them to display emotion through the expressions on their faces and their body language; this will also enable children to develop empathy for her character. Using the language of emotion to gather some nuanced and varied responses from the children, drawing on some of the language used in the zone of relevance where appropriate, would further support them to articulate their thoughts and prepare them for future writing. While they are showing their freeze frame, you could also ask them to explain how they are feeling and what they are thinking. This works particularly well if you are able to deepen their responses by asking questions which encourage developing their answer further. For example, 'I feel joyful.', 'Why do you feel joyful?', 'I'm joyful because I am touching the soft grass with my feet for the first time'.

- This will enable deeper connections to the character and therefore the children will be better placed to write. When they have explored a fictional situation through talk or role play, they will often be ready to write in role as a character in the story. Taking the role of a particular character is particularly supportive for developing writers as it enables them to see events from a different viewpoint and involves them writing in a different voice. In a role, children can also often access feelings and language that are not available to them when they write as themselves. Offering the children the opportunity to write in role as Rapunzel and to reflect her experiences and viewpoint at this point in the story will enable them to decide for themselves how to reveal her personality through their writing choices. For example, writing with confidence rather than anxiety or anguish about her escape for the tower and expressing her happiness at being outside for the first time. Before the children write in role, it would be helpful to give the class time to look over all the different work completed, such as the Role on the Wall and the language generated in the zone of relevance work.

- Once the children have been given sustained writing time to plan, draft and write, you could read their writing aloud, exploring how Rapunzel is different in this version of the story from the traditional version. For example, reflecting on her active role as the one who finds her way out of the tower and the absence of another character whose role it is to 'save' her.

TEACHING READING STRATEGIES: SHARED AND GROUP READING

Within a balanced reading programme there will be time dedicated to varied reading experiences, including opportunities for the teacher to model reading skills and strategies: predicting, sampling, confirming, self-monitoring and self-correcting, and demonstrating the full range of cueing systems, semantic, syntactic and grapho-phonic, as well as 'thinking aloud' or making the implicit, explicit. This time should also aim to continue to foster positive reading attitudes and maintain children's confidence in reading.

Shared reading offers the perfect opportunity for teachers to model how they can use a range of strategies when reading, and to articulate this 'thinking aloud' so that the children can hear and understand what applying different reading strategies looks like in practice. Shared reading can occur either as a whole class or in small groups. Having enlarged copies of texts such as 'big books' and photocopied extracts will ensure the children get the most out of shared reading sessions, as well as using homemade versions of well known or traditional tales as well as books made by the class.

Shared reading is an ideal opportunity for children to apply grapho-phonic knowledge in context and for teaching to facilitate focusing analytically on print. This will include the recognition of written language as units, such as words within words, rime, syllables and common spelling patterns, rather than only individual graphemes and phonemes.

Teachers can draw attention, for example, to the principles of 'onset and rime' in shared and group reading sessions. Onset and rime are the letters before and after a vowel:

S/and   **r**/ing   **m**/eet   **l**/ook

B/and   **s**/ing   **sh**/eet   **b**/ook

Gr/and   **br**/ing   **str**/eet   **sh**/ook

Dividing words into onset and rime helps children to make the link between how words are said and how they are written down.

"DIVIDING WORDS INTO ONSET AND RIME HELPS CHILDREN TO MAKE THE LINK BETWEEN HOW WORDS ARE SAID AND HOW THEY ARE WRITTEN DOWN."

Rime also allows children to see the relationships between words. For example, recognising and making analogies between words with the same rime (*dog* and *fog*, *hand* and *grand*) helps children to begin to classify groups of words and so build up a significant repertoire. As children's reading vocabulary increases, they are able to draw on more examples and make more analogies, in reading and also in spelling (O'Sullivan, 2007).

After having read and enjoyed a high quality text such as *How to Find Gold* by Viviane Schwarz you could choose a selection of key words from the book to demonstrate this strategy, such as map, sunk, plank and sack. Discuss with the children how they might use what they know about how words are formed to be able to read them. After modelling, invite the children to explore how many words they might be able to devise using the principle of onset and rime. For example, if I know how to read and spell 'sack' I can apply the same principles to read and spell the words back, crack, hack, tack, black, Jack, shack, stack, track, rack, pack etc. Once the children feel that they have exhausted their options, encourage them to sense check their words using a dictionary.

Children can then continue to apply this with other unknown words independently, making predictions based on words that they do know. You can also build a class collection of onsets and rimes which you could display, ensuring you draw attention to the patterns and analogies. This will support your developing readers towards reading more fluently.

Poetry collections and anthologies are particularly supportive in moving children towards reading fluency and for many children poetry is their 'route into reading'. The rhythms and patterns of poetry introduce children to a range of reading skills, and as they naturally pick up rhymes and rhythms they want to join in. A rich experience of hearing and learning poems is therefore a fantastic way of learning how language works.

Out and About by Shirley Hughes makes for the perfect collection to explore in Key Stage 1. In this book of poetry, the seasons are seen from a child's eye view. Each section opens with a glorious double-page spread showing families engaged in a range of seasonally specific activities, such as playing on the sand in summer and sledging and snowballing in winter. This poetry therefore has strong links to the outdoor environment as well as childhood seasonal experiences:

- Consider planning wider curriculum experiences alongside this text and the time of year that you share and enjoy the poems, to make sure that children have ample opportunities to explore their natural surroundings, engage with the seasonal elements, and have sensory experiences related to themes in the book. This will support the children in understanding and using the expressive and figurative language used in the poems authentically, and in turn to write expressively about things they see, do and experience in the outdoor environment, appropriate to the current season.

- Taking as an example three poems from the collection *Mudlarks, Water and Sand*, you can find opportunities for supporting early phonological development and building children's vocabulary, as well as looking at the basic and complex code, within the exploration and enjoyment of the poetry.

- Prior to teaching specific strategies it would be invaluable to open up an appropriate area outdoors for children to be involved in exploratory play with mud, sand and water. Allowing lots of time for open-ended sensory play, including exploring the differences in the sensory experience when mud and sand are dry and when they are wet, and when water is warm and cold, will enable the children to make self-to-text connections when you come to read the poems. While the children are exploring, encourage them to share language to describe their experiences, talk about their experiences in reference to their senses, and make videos to capture the language used or to note down the language used as you observe the children at play. You can then draw on and build on this language when you come to read the poems.

- Following this you can read and explore each poem in turn. Reading each through, at least twice, before asking the children to discuss how it makes them feel and what experiences in the poem compared with their own experiences with mud, water and sand, will support their understanding and enjoyment. In each poem in turn, highlight the particular words and phrases that help the reader to get a picture of what mud, water and sand are like, and why this child likes them, for example, the alliterative words and phrases that have onomatopoeic qualities in *Mudlarks*.

- Looking more closely at the words in the poem would also provide some groups with an opportunity to use and apply phonic learning, investigating and using the 'sl' consonant cluster in context, with words like slippy, sloppy, slap, slither and slide as well as the word slosh in the poem *Water*. You could also look here at wider verbs to describe actions with water like slosh, spray and paddle, thus extending the children's ability to connect with the actions they made during the play and being able to describe these.
- This wordplay and exploration, which is one of the most basic pleasures of poetry, gives the opportunity for playing games with language so that the shapes, sounds and rhythms of words are enjoyed as well as their meaning. And this is key to developing your young readers' fluency.

GROUP READING

Reading in a group can also provide an opportunity to give specific children targeted support and extend the children's independence and deepen comprehension. Books such as *Rabbit and Bear Attack of the Snack* by Julian Gough and Jim Field help to facilitate a deeper, inferential response to texts as well as the possibility to create links to well-known stories and make those intertextual connections explicit for young readers.

The book is the third in a series about an unlikely and entertaining friendship between a rabbit and a bear. Rabbit is hot-headed and jumps to conclusions about an owl that has landed in their midst; he whips up mass hysteria and a bit of a frenzy about the danger this owl poses to the animals in the forest, resulting in the owl being put in a cage. By the end of the book Bear helps him to see reason and so Rabbit not only develops as a character but also shows the reader that good friends will allow you to redeem yourself. Those familiar with *Winnie the Pooh* will already be able to draw comparisons between this story and the chapter 'When Kanga and Baby Roo come to the Forest', in which Rabbit is also very suspicious of the new arrivals and tries to make the other animals frightened of them.

You could therefore examine these connections by reading both stories with the group and using the 'double bubble' approach so that the children can compare the two characters. To do this, place the characters in the centre of the paper, next to each other; you could use images to support this. Then work together to establish in the centre of the two characters the similarities that the characters share, such as 'they are both suspicious of the new animal'. Then to the left of both the characters you can establish the differences between the characters. As you continue to read the books you can continue to revisit the 'double bubble' to see if the similarities have grown or not.

SUPPORTING INDEPENDENT READING

'As with any skills learnt, children need opportunities for individual reading to practise and consolidate their learning. Time needs to be built into the school day for children to read and enjoy books independently' (Elborn, 2015: 31).

This will need to include directed independent reading time, such as in group reading time where children may re-read or read on in the group text by themselves, where they may be investigating non-fiction texts linked to the wider curriculum or to other books they are reading, or they may be preparing responses to reading in readiness for further dialogic talk or preparing questions about reading for a friend.

There also needs to be time for children to engage in undirected free voluntary reading; this means choosing material of their own choice and providing time for sustained periods of quiet, uninterrupted reading. Ensuring that children have dedicated time to explore, browse and self-select from a well-stocked, inviting and accessible reading environment, including access to a growing variety of digital and multimodal texts, will make this free voluntary reading time as valuable as possible.

Having a core selection of known and unknown books that enthuse children and encourage avid reading is therefore essential to developing children who want to read often, widely, and for pleasure. In the first instance, as you build and develop this collection, you will need to know what appeals to the children in your class. Regularly seeking pupil voice and talking to the children about the books that they like and dislike, as well as talking to their parents about their reading habits and preferences, will support you to fine-tune this provision.

Books by popular authors, and based around themes and topics that you know will interest your children, are a great starting point for supporting them to branch out into independent reading. Books in a series work particularly well as children enjoy the comfort of returning to the familiarity of the known characters and settings, as well as engaging in the 'book gossip' and talk that comes with sharing books that it is likely their friends and peers are also enjoying. If you have already enjoyed a book together as a class or group, having the following books in the series available in your class reading areas will encourage this. Series such as the *Claude* books by Alex T. Smith are an excellent example which would enhance any Key Stage 1 book stock.

Some of the children in Key Stage 1 may still be at the start of their reading journey, and these early readers will need books for independent reading that will not only support them to practise lifting the words off the page but will also allow them to see themselves as readers and engage in readerly behaviours. This is where collections such as the CLPE's *Learning to Read* collection can support you to have a selection of books which will ensure you are providing independent materials that will facilitate the children to apply their growing reading skills and strategies, but will also enable them to explore rich texts and develop their comprehension and inference skills at the same time.

On the other hand, many of the children in Key Stage 1 will be reading independently with confidence for more sustained periods. These children are likely to move between familiar and unfamiliar texts in their reading choices, linking new texts to others read and to personal experiences, and this is to be encouraged and supported.

These readers, who are developing confidence in tackling new kinds of texts independently and showing evidence of growing enthusiasm for a wider range of reading material that they self-select, should have available to them information books, longer picture books, comics, graphic novels, age-appropriate newspapers, short chapter books and a range of digital texts, as the range of reading materials in your classroom should encourage these children to broaden their reading experiences.

As an example, in the book *Azzi in Between* Sarah Garland uses a comic strip format to tell the story of Azzi who has to flee her own country with her parents, leaving her grandmother behind, and settle as a refugee in a new country. The format of this book would therefore offer a challenge to those readers who are developing their experience of a wider range of texts, but the content of the book would also prompt them to develop a deeper response to the themes and issues.

Finally, encouraging peer recommendation and making links with bookshops and libraries that can further the children's engagement in books will make all the difference in sustaining

Key Stage 1 children's motivation beyond their acquisition of the basic skills of reading. Ultimately, knowing your young readers and being a reading teacher yourself will support you to make the best recommendations that are best suited to each individual.

REFERENCES

Barrs, M. and Cork, V. (2001) *The Reader in the Writer*. London: CLPE.

CLPE (1991) *The Reading Book*. London: CLPE.

CLPE (2016) *The Reading and Writing Scales*. London: CLPE.

Elborn, S. (2015) *Handbook of Teaching Early Reading: More Than Phonics*. UKLA.

Chambers, A. (2011) *Tell Me: Children, Reading and Talk with the Reading Environment*. Stroud: The Thimble Press.

Cremin, T. et al. (2014) *Building Communities of Engaged Readers: Reading for Pleasure*. Abingdon: Routledge.

Krashen, S. (2004) *The Power of Reading*. London: Heinemann.

O'Sullivan, O. and Thomas, A. (2007) *Understanding Spelling*. Abingdon: Routledge.

FIND OUT MORE

A comprehensive selection of high-quality books for children from ages three to eleven https://clpe.org.uk/corebooks

Choosing and Using Quality Children's Texts: What We Know Works https://clpe.org.uk/library-and-resources/what-we-know-works-booklets/choosing-and-using-quality-childrens-texts-what-we

The Power of Reading: Building a Text-based English Curriculum https://clpe.org.uk/powerofreading

CHILDREN'S BOOKS REFERENCED IN THIS CHAPTER

Atinuke and Tobia, L. (2012) *Anna Hibiscus*. London: Walker.

Brown, R. (2012) *A Dark Dark Tale*. London: Andersen Press.

Cooper, H. (1999) *Pumpkin Soup*. London: Corgi.

Fearnley, J. (2008) *Mr Wolf and the Enormous Turnip*. London: Egmont.

Garland, S. (2013) *Azzi in Between*. London: Frances Lincoln.

Gough, J. and Field, J. (2018) *Rabbit and Bear Attack of the Snack*. London: Hodder.

Hughes, S. (2016) *Out and About*. London: Walker.

Milne, A. A., Shephard, E.H. (2016) *Winnie-the-Pooh*. London: Egmont.

Schwarz, V. (2017) *How to Find Gold*. London: Walker.

Smith, A.T. (2011) *Claude in the City*. London: Hodder Children's Books.

Soundar, C. and Lessac, F. (2018) *Pattan's Pumpkin*. London: Otter-Barry Books.

Tolstoy, A. and Sharkey, N. (2005) *The Gigantic Turnip*. London: Barefoot Books.

Woollvin, B. (2018) *Rapunzel*. London: Two Hoots.

CHAPTER 14

DEVELOPING A RICH READING APPROACH IN YEAR 3 AND 4

DARREN MATTHEWS AND LOUISE JOHNS-SHEPHERD

In Year 3 and 4, as children transition from Key Stage 1, teachers continue to have an enormously important role in supporting children's developing reading and writing identity. Children's implicit and explicit knowledge of language, vocabulary and grammar should be continually stretched through the quality, breadth and range of texts being read aloud, reread, discussed and performed. Through social engagement around high-quality texts and through the rich discussions which ensue, children are able to think increasingly about the pragmatic choices made by professional writers and the effect those choices might have upon the reader.

"ENGAGEMENT WITH HIGH QUALITY TEXTS PROMPTS RICH DISCUSSIONS SUPPORTING CHILDREN TO THINK INCREASINGLY ABOUT THE PRAGMATIC CHOICES MADE BY PROFESSIONAL WRITERS AND THE EFFECT THESE CHOICES MIGHT HAVE UPON THE READER."

Children will be contextualising conversations around language based on what they have had the opportunity to read, hear, say, and write.

For all of these reasons and more, the quality and diversity of the texts which children have access to are central to the school reading curriculum and there need to be plenty of opportunities for children to access a range of texts through independent reading for pleasure, group reading, and being read to by an adult. One of the crucial responsibilities of the classroom practitioner in Year 3/4 is to continue to expound, exemplify and embody the central importance of reading for pleasure. Ensure there is a vibrant reading environment, access to a range of texts, and that adults working in the classroom have a good knowledge of texts so that they can broaden and extend children's reading experiences, making sure that they are able to build on their own interests and come across a range of authors, illustrators, poets, and text types.

Children are developing their independence as readers in Year 3 and 4 and teachers will want to ensure that they have both the time and the book stock to support independent reading. This could be directed or supported independent reading where children can re-read a familiar class book, use books to research wider curriculum learning, or take part in activities such as close reading or text marking. There will also need to be opportunities for free, voluntary reading where children who are developing their independence have the time and space to read without the need for a specific response or 'activity', just as mature readers do when they are reading for pleasure. They will then be in a position to continue to develop their own knowledge of texts, their likes, dislikes, tastes, and preferences.

If all of this is in place in the Year 3/4 classroom then children will have a positive view of reading and will be encouraged to build their reading stamina, broadening their experience, and developing and building their vocabulary, and continue their journey to becoming lifelong readers and writers with all of the benefits this brings.

READING ALOUD

Reading aloud continues to be important in the Year 3/4 classroom, even though it is likely that the majority of children will also be able to read to themselves independently. Reading aloud allows even experienced readers the opportunity to access the text at a different level: as the text is read aloud they do not have to process the transition from symbols on the page to words to sentences to visual images, and thus the journey is much more immediate and so more of the mind can be focused on the emotional and intellectual response. Having a model of a fluent expressive reader and the shared communal enjoyment of a story or a poem (a shared fear, a shared laugh, a shared cry) is a hugely important moment, and really emphasises the social aspects of enjoying and sharing a great story. As with all reading aloud experiences (at home, at school, in a library), balancing new and familiar texts, as well as balancing books chosen by the audience with books chosen by the reader, is hugely important.

Allowing the class to have some level of ownership over this precious time is vital, and it may be that you would give your class the opportunity to vote on the next read-aloud book they want, or to suggest or recommend titles they think that the whole class would enjoy together.

Make sure that children understand that returning to books that they have heard read aloud can be a pleasurable experience.

> **"MAKE SURE THAT CHILDREN UNDERSTAND THAT RETURNING TO BOOKS THAT THEY HAVE HEARD READ ALOUD CAN BE A PLEASURABLE EXPERIENCE."**

Keep a box or small shelf of books that celebrate 'books we have enjoyed together' that children can access independently or that you can return to occasionally as a whole class. Keep a shared record of your class reading journey in a whole class reading journal or on a display board.

You will also want to ensure that you are reading aloud a balance of materials. As well as a well-chosen novel you would also want to build in sufficient time to read poetry, traditional tales and picture books.

BOOKS TO READ ALOUD WITH YEAR 3 AND 4

Try picture books or poetry with repetition, chiming in, pattern and rhyme, books which play with language and use it to create interest or humour. Michael Rosen's *Quick Let's Get Out of Here* or his *Big Book of Bad Things* are great examples of this.

Picture books continue to be important in KS2. Children will often see things in picture books at this age that they may have missed at an earlier stage. For example, many of Anthony Browne's books have complex themes and many layers of meaning that really appeal to children of this age. Almost wordless books like Jeannie Baker's *Belonging* are also very powerful books to share.

Traditional tales help children understand the 'big shapes' of storytelling and the importance of devices like repetition and patterning. Lari Don's *Tales of Wisdom and Wonder* or *The Lion and the Unicorn* by Jane Ray are great read-aloud texts.

Reading aloud models the shapes and patterns of storytelling for children, as does the oral storytelling tradition. When you can, it is great to learn some short stories by heart to tell children. This helps them develop their knowledge of traditional tales, standard story structures and then make intertextual connections. Listening to a 'told' story is also a very different experience from listening to a read story, so this adds a different and interesting dimension to the shared story time.

Lower Key Stage 2 is a great point to introduce longer novels where children can become caught up in the story and emotionally invested in characters. Modern stories like *Varjak Paw* by S.F. Said or Onjali Rauf's *The Boy at the Back of the Class* work really well with this age group, as do classics such as *Charlotte's Web* or *Pippi Longstocking*. This is also an ideal opportunity to introduce series to children; reading aloud the first in a series such as Lemony Snicket's *Series of Unfortunate Events*, or the *Ottoline* stories by Chris Riddell, can give confident readers a starting point and help them discover new favourites.

WORKING WITH A BOOK IN MORE DEPTH

Choosing books which offer wider learning opportunities – a book which stimulates wide and engaging discussion, deepens reading responses, makes connections with a web of reading experience and world experience, prompts questions and curiosity and passion, and will give an opportunity for writing and other creative work. *The Wild Robot* by Peter Brown has a carefully crafted narrative structure and the characters and settings are well drawn, offering young readers a good model for their own story planning and descriptive writing. The characterisation and setting are supported by a wealth of illustration which can be explored and discussed alongside the text. The well-paced story and emotional depth of the characters make this book ideal for whole-class work.

IDEAS FOR WORKING WITH *THE WILD ROBOT* BY PETER BROWN

- When starting this book with a class, you might initially keep back the title and cover from the children so that they are able to respond to the text alone, and early discussions will involve them developing strategies of prediction, close reading, clarification and visualisation. Even from the start, the author's choice of narrative voice immediately involves the reader describing a violent storm and its aftermath. The teacher begins with reading this rich language aloud and allowing children to respond by sharing their own emotional response, as well as their visualisation of what that opening description meant to them. This then provides the ideal open and inclusive opportunity to begin to consider author intention and the careful choice of language by returning to the text in small groups to consider what in the author's craft has inspired their own unique visualisation.
- Children can then predict what might be found within those mysterious and endangered wooden crates before the rest of the chapter is read and the robots are revealed. As with many great children's novels, Peter Brown's story might be used to stimulate wider curricular activity. Where this is done in an authentic and meaningful way, it can support children's understanding of character, circumstance or setting; it can support preparation and purpose for writing; and it can provide a great stimulus for further independent reading. For example, at this early stage in the story, we might explore either in groups or as a whole class what we currently know about robots and what we might like to find out. The class may be able to draw together a rich web of robot characters from different fictional worlds – books, comics, TV and film – as well as how robots are currently used in the real world and how scientists, engineers and programmers think that they may be incorporated into life in the near and distant futures. This will provide an ideal opportunity to teach children how to read and navigate different kinds of information texts in small groups or independently. A research area could be created in the classroom or school library in which high-quality books, magazines and perhaps tablets loaded with appropriate digital texts and websites could be attractively displayed and accessed with increasing confidence by the children. Home/school collaboration could be encouraged in providing opportunities for families to engage in the research and children to share new sources of information with each other, discussing its user-friendliness and authenticity.
- The next few chapters of this heavily illustrated novel introduce further key characters which can be directly compared with Roz the robot. What different viewpoints might the groups of characters have? What might the otters be thinking? What about the robot? As these creatures of the natural world of the island and the robot start interacting with each other, the children can start to draw together their early thoughts about what the big

shape of this story could be. What might the story be about? What kind of story could it be? These types of questions allow children to draw on their own existing knowledge of story, genre, theme and structure without worrying about being wrong. Crucially, we aren't asking them to summarise what has happened and accurately predict the rest of the book – an impossible and pointless request – we are instead asking them to suggest what could happen and, reflecting as a reader, what they might have experienced that has led them to this possibility.

- As they progress with the narrative, children can work together to summarise what they know so far about Roz. Using Role on the Wall, the class can record her behaviour as well as her characteristics. Children can be encouraged to explicitly link their inferences with actual behaviour as well as drawing on the language of the text used to describe her and her interactions with the animals she meets.

- As their exploration of the book progresses, children can add more to Roz's Role on the Wall and use this to stimulate broader, philosophical discussions around Roz's 'thinking', i.e. that which is programmed and that which is learned.

- As the island's wildlife are introduced and described by the author, the class can take the opportunity to use metalanguage in context to unpick the sentence structure adopted in which the animal's action or movement is described as well as the impact of Brown's language choices, e.g. the precise and evocative verb choice (rather than unnecessary use of adjectives for the subject) and detail is provided through an adverbial phrase. Brown has then used sentence repetition to create impact, i.e. to demonstrate how the 'island was teeming with life' as Roz notices each animal one after the other.

- As Roz the Robot begins to create a home for herself on the island, prompts can be used to elicit deeper responses relating to authorial intent and enable the children to make connections to wider human themes being played out in the world around them regarding belonging and what 'home' means. *As far as Roz knows, she is home. Do you agree? Will the animals agree that this is the robot's home? Where do we think Roz belongs? Who does she belong to? What makes you think that? What does home mean to Roz? What does it mean to you?* Children may also explore the fundamental concept of 'home' in order to deepen understanding and empathy.

- As the class's deep understanding of the character grows they will be more confident and able to write in role from Roz's point of view, perhaps regularly recording her new experiences in her log or writing to Roz offering advice when she comes up against a further challenge to her survival in the wild.

- After reading aloud the section when Roz properly meets the island's many animal inhabitants, ask the children to respond to the language they have heard. *What do descriptions like 'monster', 'unnatural', 'mysterious creature' tell us about how the animals are feeling about having Roz on the island? How do you feel about the way in which the animals are treating 'our robot'? How would you feel if you were one of the animals? How would you feel if you were the newcomer?* Role play could be used to delve further into the animals' responses to Roz at this moment, with children drawing on either the text or their own inferences to decide what they would say in role as their chosen animals and how they would say it. The children can whisper their 'gossip' to a neighbouring animal until all are interacting in this way. You might start each round with another fearmongering statement selected from the text.

- Classroom drama techniques can also be used to effectively delve into moments depicted in the illustration as well as through the text. For example, the moment in which Roz and the gosling meet – a relationship that will become particularly important to both characters' arcs. Ask the children to work in small groups, responding to the illustration of this moment: *What do you think the gosling is thinking? What do you think Roz is thinking in this moment? From whose viewpoint are we looking? How does it make us feel about the gosling?* After an initial response, pairs of children can be invited to reproduce the relationship from the illustration as a freeze frame. This can then be gradually brought to life using first thought tracking and then a short improvised dialogue or role play between the characters. Encourage children to draw on what we know of Roz from our wider reading, role play, and Role on the Wall work as well as the illustration prompt in deciding how she might react to this gosling. Any enactment could subsequently be recorded using speech and/or thought bubbles around a copy of the illustration, or even the development of a short comic strip retelling of the moment.

TEACHING READING STRATEGIES: SHARED AND GROUP READING

As part of the reading programme in their classroom, alongside working on a book in depth as a whole class and the time given to reading aloud outside of those sessions, the teacher will also be dedicating time to sequences of activities which target specific reading skills and strategies designed to improve reading fluency, comprehension and reader response. Because of the wide range of experiences and needs in a Year 3/4 classroom, these books are likely to be selected slightly differently from those read aloud by the teacher in whole-class lessons.

Teachers will choose texts that give opportunities to model and teach strategies targeted at supporting the specific stages in children's reading journeys.

"CHOOSE TEXTS THAT GIVE OPPORTUNITIES TO MODEL AND TEACH STRATEGIES TARGETED AT SUPPORTING THE SPECIFIC STAGES IN CHILDREN'S READING JOURNEYS."

These strategies might include predicting, clarifying, and summarising as well as returning to identified sections of text for close reading, skimming and scanning. The teacher will also be able to use this time to support the children in building independence and reading stamina, explicitly demonstrating a full range of cueing systems and self-monitoring strategies.

If these reading sessions are being taught in small groups, this might also provide children with the opportunity to select the text that they would like to explore together. The teacher might suggest three or four potential titles, all within a reasonable distance of the children's ability to read independently, from which they could browse, discuss and eventually select the title which interests them the most, thereby empowering the group and giving them control over their own reading journey.

These reading sessions are an ideal opportunity for children to practise and apply their strategies for decoding and defining unfamiliar vocabulary, whether this is through applying their phonemic knowledge, or drawing on larger units of language, e.g. syllabification, common prefixes or suffixes, comparison with familiar words, onset and rime, etc. Within their groups, children can support each other with defining unfamiliar vocabulary, either through sharing experiences, their individual knowledge of the world, or by drawing on the context of the sentence, paragraph, character or setting, or through researching an appropriately phrased definition.

Teachers of children at this stage may well want to refer to the free CLPE Reading Scales which help you to think about next steps for readers at different stages of development. It is essential that adults know a variety of texts suitable for children at this age and stage. The CLPE Core Book site highlights a range of suitable texts.

Some examples of texts that we know work well for developing and moderately fluent readers in this age group are listed below:

Suggestions of Texts for Developing Readers	
The Puffin Book of Fantastic First Poems edited by June Crebbin	Poetry collection
Hairy Maclary from Donaldson's Dairy by Lynley Dodd	Rhyming text
Would You Rather by John Burningham	Supportive illustrations and strong tune – opportunity for deeper response
I Love My New Toy by Mo Willems	Decodable text and supportive illustrations
Grace and Family by Mary Hoffman and Caroline Binch	Opportunities for deeper response
Egg by Alex T. Smith	Opportunities for deeper response – links with traditional tales
The Story Tree: Tales to be Read Aloud retold by Hugh Lupton and Sophie Fatus	Traditional tale
The Lonely Penguin by Petr Horacek	Decodable text – story with supportive illustrations
The Emperor's Egg by Martin Jenkins and Jane Chapman	Non-fiction
Peas, Please! by Fiona Macdonald	Non-fiction – real life experiences
Cheese Belongs to You by Alexis Deacon	Decodable text and supportive illustrations

Suggestions of Texts for Moderately Fluent Readers	
A Caribbean Dozen edited by John Agard and Grace Nichols	Poetry collection
The Snail and the Whale by Julia Donaldson and Axel Sheffler	Rhyming text
Peas and Tickles by Kes Gray and Nick Sharratt	Chapter book with supportive illustrations
Claude in the Country by Alex T. Smith	Chapter book with supportive illustrations
The Castle in the Field by Michael Morpurgo	Chapter book with supportive illustrations
The Colour of Home by Mary Hoffman and Karin Littlewood	Opportunities for deeper response
Hermelin by Mini Grey	Opportunities for deeper response

(Continued)

(Continued)

Suggestions of Texts for Moderately Fluent Readers	
The Princess and the White Bear King by Tanya Robyn Batt and Nicoletta Ceccoli	Extended traditional tale
Cinderella by David Wood and Shahab Shamshirsaz	Familiar traditional tale
The World Came to My Place Today by Jo Readman and Ley Honor Roberts	Non-fiction – intertextual
Thinker: My Puppy Poet and Me by Eloise Greenfield and Ehsan Abdollahi	Poetry

SUPPORTING INDEPENDENT READING

As well as time allocated within the school reading programme to deepen response and to directly teach reading skills and strategies, children will also need time to consolidate and practise these skills independently as well as to read books that they have chosen themselves. The range of books that children read will obviously be dictated by their own tastes and preferences as well as recommendations from adults and other children. However, some examples of books that we know work particularly well for fluent, independent readers at this age include:

A Boy and a Bear in a Boat by Dave Shelton	Humour and illustration
Paddington at Work by Michael Bond	Series
Emil and the Detectives by Erich Kastner	'Classic'
All About Me by Michael Rosen	Non-fiction
Angry Arthur by Hiawyn Oram	Picture book
Bananas in My Ears by Michael Rosen	Poetry
A Walk in Paris by Salvatore Rubbino	Non-fiction
Knights and Bikes by Gabrielle Kent	Adventure story
The No.1 Car Spotter by Atinuke	Series
The Rainmaker Danced by John Agard and Satoshi Kitamura	Poetry
Hilda and the Troll by Luke Pearson	Graphic novel

CHILDREN'S BOOKS REFERENCED IN THIS CHAPTER

Agard, J. and Kitamura, S. (2017) *The Rainmaker Danced*. London: Hodder Children's Books.
Agard, J. and Nichols, G. (2011) *A Caribbean Dozen: Poems from 12 Caribbean Poets*. London: Walker.
Atinuke (2010) *The No.1 Car Spotter*. London: Walker Books.
Baker, J. (2008) *Belonging*. London: Walker Books.
Batt, T.R. and Ceccoli, N. (2008) *The Princess and the White Bear King*. London: Barefoot Books.

Bond, M. (1966) *Paddington at Work*. Glasgow: HarperCollins Children's Books.

Brown, P. (2018) *The Wild Robot*. London: Piccadilly Press.

Burningham, J. (1999) *Would You Rather…* London: Red Fox.

Crebbin, J (2006) *The Puffin Book of Fantastic First Poems*. London: Puffin.

Deacon, A. and Schwarz, V. (2014) *Cheese Belongs to You*. London: Walker Books.

Dodd, L. (1983) *Hairy Maclary from Donaldson's Dairy*. London: Puffin.

Donaldson, J. and Scheffler, A. (2004) *The Snail and the Whale*. London: Macmillan.

Gray, K. and Sharratt, N. (2013) *Peas and Tickles*. London: Red Fox.

Greenfield, E. and Abdollahi, E. (2018) *Thinker: My Puppy Poet and Me*. London: Tiny Owl.

Grey, M. (2015) *Hermelin, the Detective Mouse*. London: Red Fox.

Hoffman, M. and Binch C. (2012) *Grace and Family*. London: Frances Lincoln.

Hoffman, M. and Littlewood, K. (2012) *The Colour of Home*. London: Frances Lincoln.

Horáček, P. (2012) *The Lonely Penguin*. London: Collins Big Cat.

Jenkins, M. and Chapman, J. (2015) *The Emperor's Egg*. London: Walker Books.

Kästner, E. (1959) *Emil and the Detectives*. London: Puffin Books.

Kent, G. (2018) *Knights and Bikes*. London: Knights Of.

Lindgren A. and Child, L. (2010) *Pippi Longstocking*. Oxford: Oxford University Press.

Lupton, H. and Fatus, S. (2009) *The Story Tree: Tales to be Read Aloud*. London: Barefoot Books.

Lupton, H. and Sharkey N. (1998) *Tales of Wisdom and Wonder*. Oxford: Barefoot Books.

Macdonald, F. (2011) *Peas, Please!* London: Collins Big Cat.

Morpurgo, M. (2013) *The Castle in the Field*. Edinburgh: Barrington Stoke.

Oram, H. and Kitamura, S. (2008) *Angry Arthur*. London: Andersen Press.

Pearson, L. (2013) *Hilda and the Troll*. London: Flying Eye Books.

Rauf, O. (2018) *The Boy at the Back of the Class*. London: Orion Books.

Ray, J. (2017) *The Lion and the Unicorn and other Hairy Tales*. New York: Boxer Books.

Readman, J. and Roberts, L.H. (2004) *The World Came to My Place Today*, Eden Project.

Riddell, C. (2007) *Ottoline and the Yellow Cat*. London: Macmillan.

Rosen, M. (1985) *Quick Let's Get Out of Here*. London: Puffin.

Rosen, M. (2010) *Michael Rosen's Big Book of Bad Things*. London: Puffin.

Rosen, M. (2015) *Michael Rosen: All About Me*. London: Collins Big Cat.

Rosen, M. and Blake, Q. (2011) *Bananas in My Ears*. London: Walker.

Rubbino, S. (2015) *A Walk in Paris*. London: Walker.

Said, S.F. and McKean, D. (2003) *Varjak Paw*. Oxford: David Fickling Books.

Shelton, D. (2014) *A Boy and a Bear in a Boat*. New York: Yearling.

Smith, A.T. (2011) *Egg*. London: Hodder Children's Books.

Smith, A.T. (2012) *Claude in the Country.,* London: Hodder Children's Books.

Snicket, L. (1999) *A Series of Unfortunate Events: The Bad Beginning*. London: Egmont.

White, E.B. (1963) *Charlotte's Web*. London: Puffin.

Willems, M. (2013) *I Love My New Toy*. London: Walker.

Wood, D. and Shamshirsaz, S. (2017) *Cinderella*. Glasgow: Collins.

CHAPTER 15

DEVELOPING A RICH READING APPROACH IN YEAR 5 AND 6

DR JONNY RODGERS

INTRODUCTION

More than any other Key Stage, Upper Key Stage 2 (UKS2) enjoys a pivotal perspective, looking both forwards and backwards. Of course, if education is a journey from ignorance to wisdom, from dependence to independence, all students from EYFS to Year 13 will look back to where they have come from, as well as ahead to where they are going. But the last two years of their primary education represent for the pupils in this chapter the culmination of all that has been learned since joining school, an almost indescribably giant leap from being unable to read or write or express themselves orally except to express the most basic needs, to the mastery of a range of cognitively sophisticated and inter-related skills straddling reading, writing, speaking and listening. Furthermore the acquisition, consolidation and application of these skills go hand-in-hand with a range of attitudes and approaches that can set them on the path to lifelong learning: mastery brings a mindset.

These years also see pupils marshalling and orchestrating all these skills, strategies and attitudes as they move on to KS3 and all that secondary school requires of them. English as it is taught in the secondary phase by a subject specialist is likely to differ greatly from what they might be used to from their primary classroom with their generalist classroom teacher. Yet as primary teacher and school inspector George Sampson wrote almost a century ago, 'Teachers seem to think that it is always some other person's work to look after English. But every teacher is a teacher of English because every teacher is a teacher in English. That second sentence should be written in letters of gold over every school doorway. (Sampson, 1922: 25). In secondary school, English is the medium of instruction and the paramount requirement to be articulate in spoken and written English gives literacy incomparable value and relevance.

"TEACHERS IN YEARS 5 AND 6 WILL BE AWARE THAT IN THE MIDST OF ALL THIS LOOKING FORWARD AND LOOKING BACKWARD, THIS IS THE VERY POINT WHERE THE BUCK STOPS."

Furthermore, the classroom teacher in Year 6 and their colleague in Year 5 will be aware that in the midst of all this looking forward and looking backward, this is the very point where the buck stops, current assessment regulations mean that all pupils sit an end of Key Stage SAT in reading comprehension and in spelling, punctuation and grammar, as well as having their writing assessed and teacher's assessment moderated. Yet regardless of prevailing assessment constraints and expectations to be secondary-ready, these two years are about establishing pupils' identity as literate citizens able to understand and make themselves understood with confidence and sophistication in the world they are about to enter.

Catering to the needs of UKS2 learners can be a double-edged sword, however. Certainly, the six or seven years of schooling they draw on give pupils in Years 5 and 6 the greatest experience of any in the primary phase of the artistic, creative and dramatic approaches already outlined in previous chapters: these pupils are the most fully versed in the different remits of editing partners and response partners; they have stood clear from the reassuring scaffolding of a Tell Me grid to frame their booktalk; they are familiar with Aidan Chambers' special as well as his basic questions; and they have taken on and mastered all the roles in Literature Circles. Yet UKS2 teachers will also be responsible for pupils who have not yet 'joined the literacy club', so need support with filling the gaps in their phonics, with improving their spelling, as well as with increasing the accuracy and range of their punctuation and grammar; they may also be reluctant readers and/or writers. Teachers may also be supporting able pupils in the 'can but don't' quadrant of Gemma Moss's attitudinal Carroll diagram, for whom motivation is an issue.

Previous chapters have championed the use of investigative, open-ended and playful teaching approaches – especially in addressing spelling and grammar – which can channel pupils' developing linguistic curiosity and creativity. Schools which have adopted this mindset such that classrooms have become communities of enquiry will see children really 'take off' in Years 5 and 6, as they gain the confidence to give free rein to their independence and risk taking. Furthermore, to quote Dr Seuss, 'The more that you learn, the more places you'll go': UKS2 sees pupils developing their awareness that what they are learning applies across the curriculum. As their experience grows there are greater opportunities for exploring intertextuality, and reading in its widest sense: making meaning not only of a variety of texts, but also of film and other media.

Fortunately, primary teachers are increasingly aware that end of Key Stage SATs are everyone's responsibility, and that children who are secondary-ready do not become so purely as a result of their experiences in Year 6, but rather these two final years are the end of a long process of growth that continues beyond primary school. Nevertheless, teachers in Year 5 and especially 6 will inevitably have an eye to statutory assessment as part of preparing their pupils for secondary school, and will need to be prepared to defend against exam preparation and 'teaching to the test' those very approaches that they know motivate their pupils and lead to high-quality outcomes in reading and writing. Keeping the faith with a rich reading curriculum entails believing that good results will naturally 'fall out' from high-quality classroom provision and pedagogy. Exam success will be a happy by-product of practices, provision and pedagogy that develop lifelong readers and writers with a strong personal voice.

READING ALOUD

Reading aloud continues to be a vital part of the palette of reading experiences to which children should have access in Years 5 and 6, regardless of the fact that many may assume children can perfectly well access the language and content of the texts they may be encountering, and are well on their way to being independent readers as defined by the CLPE scales. The reasons why reading aloud remains important are the same as those that made it such a vital component of their reading life when they were younger, which have been outlined in previous chapters but include exposure to a high-quality model of language and repeated immersion in the tunes and rhythms of an author and their writing. Trelease's finding is especially relevant here, that children's reading age lags their listening age by two years until they reach age 13 (in other words, well beyond the primary phase). This means that the Year 5 or 6 teacher offers them access to subject matter and language that they may struggle to access independently for some time; as the grammatical complexity, linguistic and lexical sophistication and challenging nature of many of the themes addressed increase, the teacher's role as gatekeeper and facilitator is critical.

Teachers should continue to share poetry: Charles Causley's *Selected Poems for Children* (illustrated by John Lawrence) is a fine example of a text children might otherwise be unlikely to encounter on their own, although Causley was a significant children's poet (and while he also wrote for adults, his work for children, as a schoolmaster, is especially accessible) whose poems are musical, with strong rhythmical patterns. A modern ballad-writer, he uses rhyme with great skill, and his poems are pleasurable both to listen to – importantly for the children – and to read aloud – equally importantly for the teacher. They can, if desired, also lead easily into performance, drama, and even into song or dance. Most of the poems in this collection tell a story, and each of these mini-narratives gives a glimpse of a human life – just enough detail is introduced to paint a picture. Having encountered them as read-alouds, children might enjoy learning some of these poems by heart as this activity enjoys a resurgence (especially at the secondary phase where they are soon to head) as they are economical, accessible and intrinsically memorable. This is a book to browse through; and children could be invited to continue reading beyond the selection here in independent reading time or guided reading.

The role of teacher as gatekeeper, facilitator and mediator made above with regard to Jim Trelease is especially true for texts like Beverley Naidoo's *The Other Side of Truth*, which exemplifies another aspect of the read-aloud programme in UKS2. This novel offers a powerful narrative with strong links to factual events, through which the teacher can support children in exploring complex emotions and hard-hitting themes. This type of experience may be one from which children are already benefiting, as teachers may be choosing in their whole-class literacy teaching to complement picture books with novels, which will require reading aloud large sections of text if the whole text is to be enjoyed – which, of course, it is! In just the same way as reading aloud as part of a Power of Reading sequence, reading such texts aloud as a whole class story will require teachers to gloss, explain, question and provide opportunities to air and challenge opinions. Aidan Chambers' booktalk approach is an excellent vehicle for this, and by this point it is to be hoped children will be very familiar with it as a scaffold for their discussions. For *The Other Side of Truth*, teachers might especially like to use Chambers' special questions, which drill down into the ramifications of setting, viewpoint, characterisation and handling of plot.

As well as poetry and novels teachers will want to include picture books in the read-aloud repertoire. (Especially within Power of Reading teaching sequences, it is also important to model the reading aloud of non-fiction texts to show their own rhythms and structures, and conventions.) Like *The Other Side of Truth*, Francesca Sanna's *The Journey* addresses powerful emotions and challenging themes, and offers opportunities to develop an insight into and appreciation of the challenges of the refugee experience, supporting the children's development of empathy, and paving the way for an exploration of the concept of the entitlement to fundamental human rights and freedoms for all. A debut picture book that won the Klaus Flugge prize, *The Journey* draws on the experiences the author-illustrator heard first-hand from recent refugees from many countries. Each spread features a carefully chosen colour palette, depicting the variety of landscapes, real and emotional, through which a family passes, escaping conflict and seeking sanctuary. The book ends on a hopeful note but makes it clear that most refugees live with continued uncertainty, even when they hope they have reached a place of safety. The text in this book is easy to read in terms of vocabulary and sentence structure, and this apparent simplicity combined with the memorable illustrations have great power to move readers of all ages, and demonstrate unequivocally that a high-quality picture book is appropriate for KS2 and beyond. One of the great strengths of the book is the intertextual connections with which it resonates, and which demand further discussion and exploration as the text is shared. As well as developing the children's visual literacy as they engage with the 'grammar' of the picturebook form, Sanna's picture book is also an effective launchpad for an exploration of news literacy, as children can focus on the bias with which many aspects of the story are handled by the media, so developing their awareness of and sensitivity to the 'fake news' agenda.

WORKiNG WiTH BOOKS iN MORE DEPTH

Previous chapters have introduced and outlined the use of an increasingly wide range of artistic, creative and dramatic teaching approaches, and the Year 5 or 6 teacher is in a privileged position to draw on these with little or no introduction or explanation, as they will be second nature to pupils in upper junior classes. It is not merely that children 'know what to do', but will also be primed to see the benefit and value of an approach when its use is called for, and can draw on previous occasions when they have used an approach to see how it can give them insights into authorial intent, characterisation or setting, personal and emotional responses to a text, or indeed whatever it is that a given approach may be designed to address. In a best-case scenario the class teacher can expect some sophistication in pupils' response to an approach, and genuine impact from using it.

To illustrate the way in which teachers can use a book-based approach to support reading in Upper Key Stage 2, three titles have been chosen as examples that we know elicit powerful responses, deep engagement and a variety of high-quality writing outcomes: William Grill's Greenaway Medal-winning picture book *Shackleton's Journey*; A.F. Harrold's *The Song from Somewhere Else* (illustrated by Levi Pinfold); and S.E. Durrant's *Running On Empty* (illustrated by Rob Biddulph).

Opportunities to explore intertextuality abound in all three texts, which also allow a wealth of cross-curricular writing, and encourage a motivated exploration of age-appropriate issues, e.g. transition and change, leadership, friendship and bullying. There is a rich vein of debate and discussion in all three titles that children will be well-equipped to respond to by this stage in their primary career.

Shackleton's Journey weaves a detailed visual narrative of Shackleton's epic journey to Antarctica, William Grill's skilful use of coloured pencils and vibrant hues evoking the adventure and excitement that surrounded the expedition. His well-researched drawings, rich with detail, fastidiously reproduce the atmosphere of the expedition, and children love examining the diagrams of the peculiar provisions and the individual drawings of each sled dog and packhorse. The book takes the academic and historical information behind the expedition and reinterprets it for a young audience, and a particularly effective approach in the classroom is for each member of the class to take on the role of one of the *Endurance*'s crew, applying for their position on the expedition, and inhabiting that historical character's experience for the duration for the voyage. Dramatic approaches including Role on the Wall, Role Play, Conscience Alley and Readers Theatre afford the children insights into human behaviour, and develop their empathy through exploring dilemmas; literally sharing the journey gives them something to say, and the language with which to say it.

Similar approaches, reinforced by Freeze Framing and Thought Tracking, are advocated to enable children to engage with the issues faced by AJ in *Running on Empty*. AJ is an eleven-year-old boy who is great at running, like his grandfather in his youth, and has dreams of competing in the Olympics one day. However, Grandad has recently died and AJ's parents, who have learning difficulties, are having problems managing money, which was something for which Grandad took responsibility. How AJ copes with his new situation, and how others in his life also learn to adjust and collaborate, is at the heart of this novel which features strong characterisation and humorous realistic dialogue.

Dramatic approaches are also advocated for the teacher sharing with their class *The Song from Somewhere Else*, a poignant, darkly comic and deeply moving story about the power of the extraordinary, and finding friendship where you least expect it. Written by the author of the critically acclaimed *The Imaginary* and *The Afterwards*, and illustrated by award-winning Levi Pinfold, the novel charts what at first seems an unlikely friendship between Francesca ('Frank') Patel and Nick Underbridge when he rescues her from bullies. Nick is ungainly and unpopular and Frank's initial response is to shun him. However, when she visits his home she is drawn to the strange music she can hear and quickly discovers otherworldly elements to Nick's life and background. Besides the dramatic approaches, children are invited to explore music and to respond to Levi Pinfold's black and white illustrations which form an integral part of this book, enhancing the sense of mystery and uncertainty. Furthermore, the model of language offered by the novel is unparalleled – Thomas Hardy characterised himself as 'a poet who wrote some novels', and A.F. Harrold may be cut from the same cloth, making his prose an excellent model for contextual teaching of grammar, vocabulary and punctuation as outlined in previous chapters.

GROUP AND GUIDED READING

Previous chapters have outlined the wide range of skills that readers use and when making meaning from a text in the Upper Key Stage 2 classroom the focus is twofold: teachers will want to make sure that children have all the individual skills that they need and also ensure that they have mastered the orchestration of the full range of skills and strategies. Not for nothing does Usha Goswami describe reading as of one of the most complex cognitive skills that humans can learn (Goswami, 2008), so it is essential to provide a varied range of reading experiences and opportunities to practise this orchestration, as well as a selection of titles that will encourage reader response.

Alongside teacher-led group guided reading the classroom may use a Literature Circles approach (Daniels, 2002), so that children can work independently on texts of their own choice with little direction. It is also important to provide opportunities for dialogic reading and co-construction of meaning, and awareness that reading is making meaning in whatever form, and can be applied to any genre.

Three titles are outlined in this section as examples of the diversity of ways in which different texts can be used to support children in group and guided sessions, ensuring that they are practising all the skills they need to become competent and independent readers. All three have been chosen because they offer very strong models of language. In *The Savage*, Dave McKean's illustrations to David Almond's almost mythical story allow children to address complex issues in the safe setting of a reading group. Not a traditional picture book as such, the illustrated novel is beautifully written like all Almond's prose, and highly engaging. The story is narrated by Blue, a boy coping with bullying in addition to recent bereavement. Blue creates the character of 'The Savage' and through telling the Savage's story and the magical way it seems to come true he finds a way of coping with his grief. The story contains many strong themes including bereavement, bullying, family love and coping with anger.

Sharon Creech's *Love That Dog* is a powerful narrative poem that explores a child's reluctance towards poetry and his development as a poet over the course of a school year. The book is highly accessible and widens pupils' understanding of what poetry is and can do – poet Benjamin Zephaniah described it as 'simply the most original book I've read for years' – inviting them to ponder the nature of writing, the experience of being taught, and about just how personal the experience of learning is.

Piers Torday's *The Last Wild* is rich in intertextual references, and is promoted here not least for this reason: as pupils move on to KS3 the ability to compare and contrast different authors and texts, and to begin to see the way in which they relate to each other, is essential. *The Last Wild* represents an excellent primer in this skill: its hero Kester lives in Spectrum Hall, an academy for challenging children. Unable to speak since separation from his parents, he unexpectedly finds he is able to communicate with a cockroach that helps him break out from his prison-like existence, launching him into a dystopian adventure with significant environmental and political themes. Like much of Torday's writing, it is rich in allusion to other authors including C.S. Lewis. Kester's story continues in *The Dark Wild* and concludes in *The Wild Beyond* – having a recommendation for pupils after they have enjoyed one text is a key skill for any classroom teacher, so for this reason as well, *The Last Wild* is a gift.

INDEPENDENT READING

A wide and deep knowledge of all types of text is essential subject knowledge for any class-room teacher, nowhere more so than in Upper Key Stage 2, where classroom teachers have the potentially life-altering responsibility of keeping children in the 'Literacy Club' against the competing temptations that technology has to offer. Teachers in Years 5 and 6 may have pupils for whom motivation is an issue: although they are able to read they rarely do so, and have not yet 'got' reading for pleasure, and all the benefits, joys and marvels that being a reader can bring.

Teachers need to be able to draw on a canon of classics to recommend, as well as newer titles, and to keep up to date may find that book awards are especially useful, including the Carnegie Medal, Klaus Flugge Prize, Branford Boase Award, and CLiPPA. The shortlists of these awards often serve the purpose of whittling down a wide field of potential recommendations to a subset that experienced readers in the form of judges have found worthy of attention. Such awards also often feature shadowing schemes which can provide a valuable focus for individuals when they come together as a group. Bear in mind also that being able to recommend across genres (e.g. novel, poetry and picture book) reinforces the message that each form has value and is appropriate. Overtly following such awards also allows teachers to continue to model independent reading themselves: to read and be seen to read a wide variety of texts sends a powerful message to every pupil.

There are so many titles to recommend for individual reading that it is invidious to select just three, so the following are offered merely as examples of what is not an exhaustive list.

Henrietta Branford's *Fire, Bed and Bone* is an outstanding and unusual atmospheric tale of the Peasant's Revolt told from the viewpoint of a dog. This device is amazingly powerful and the dog is able to make insightful comments about the society and issues of the time, in the language of the time. It can also draw children on to Daniel Pennac's *Dog*, Andy Mulligan's *Dog*, and Patricia MacLachlan's *The Poet's Dog* which uses the same device of a dog narrator.

Roger McGough's *Sensational! Poems Inspired by the Five Senses* (illustrated by Sara Fanelli) is a book of poems that are inspired by the brain and the five senses and encourages children to read, enjoy and respond to poetry, and potentially to prepare poems to read aloud and perform, and to compose poetry of their own.

As we have said throughout this book, picture books remain an important form for Year 5 and Year 6 children to read and investigate. Joanne Schwartz's *Town Is by the Sea* (illustrated by Sydney Smith) evokes a mining community by the sea where a boy describes the daily life of his family. The brief text has a slow-paced rhythm, repeating the words 'And deep down under that sea, my father is digging for coal', reflecting the centrality this has for him as he expects that one day he will carry on the family tradition of becoming a miner. A note at the end of the book indicates that the setting is the 1950s when this would very likely have been the case. The pictures are like camera shots. Sometimes they focus on details or show only part of a scene, at other times a wide-angle lens is used, especially when the sparkling sea is depicted; the interplay of text and images makes this a book to savour and revisit.

REFERENCES

Centre for Literacy in Primary Education (2016) *The Reading and Writing Scales*. London: CLPE.

Chambers, A. (2010) *Tell Me (Children, Reading and Talk)* and *The Reading Environment (How Adults Help Children Enjoy Books)*. Stroud: Thimble Press.

Daniels, H. (2002) *Literature Circles*. Portsmout, NH: Stenhouse.

Geisel, T. (=Dr Seuss) (1978) *I Can Read with My Eyes Shut!* Glasgow: HarperCollins.

Goswami, U. (2008) Reading, complexity and the brain. *Literacy*, 42 (2): 67–74.

Krashen, S. (2004) *The Power of Reading*. London: Heinemann.

Maine, F. (2015) *Dialogic Readers: Children Talking and Thinking Together about Visual Texts*. Abingdon: Routledge.

O'Sullivan, O. and Thomas, A. (2007) *Understanding Spelling*. London: CLPE.

Sampson, G. (1922) *English for the English: A Chapter on National Education*. Cambridge: CUP.

Smith, F. (1988) *Joining the Literacy Club*. New York: Random House.

Tennent, W., Reedy, D., Hobsbaum, A. and Gamble, N. (2016) *Guiding Readers – Layers of Meaning: A Handbook for Teaching Reading Comprehension to 7-11-Year-Olds*. London: UCL IoE Press.

Trelease, J. (2013) *The Read-Aloud Handbook*, 7th edition. London: Penguin.

FIND OUT MORE

A comprehensive selection of high-quality books for children from ages three to eleven: https://clpe.org.uk/corebooks

Choosing and Using Quality Children's Texts: What We Know Works https://clpe.org.uk/library-and-resources/what-we-know-works-booklets/choosing-and-using-quality-childrens-texts-what-we

The Power of Reading: Building a Text-based English Curriculum https://clpe.org.uk/powerofreading

CHILDREN'S BOOKS REFERENCED IN THIS CHAPTER

Almond, D., illustrated by D. McKean (2009) *The Savage*. London: Walker.

Branford, H. (2002) *Fire, Bed and Bone*. London: Walker.

Causley, C., illustrated by J. Lawrence (1997) *Selected Poems for Children*. Basingstoke: Macmillan.

Creech, S. (2001) *Love That Dog*. London: Bloomsbury.

Durrant, S.E. illustrated by R. Biddulph (2018) *Running on Empty*. London: Nosy Crow.

Grill, W. (2014) *Shackleton's Journey*. London: Flying Eye.

Harrold, A.F., illustrated by E. Gravett (2014) *The Imaginary*. London: Bloomsbury.

Harrold, A.F., illustrated by L. Pinfold (2016) *The Song from Somewhere Else*. London: Bloomsbury.

Harrold, A.F., illustrated by E. Gravett (2018) *The Afterwards*. London: Bloomsbury.

MacLachlan, P., Illustrated by K. Pak (2017) *The Poet's Dog*. London: Pushkin Press.

McGough, R., illustrated by S. Fanelli (2005) *Sensational! Poems Inspired by the Five Senses*. Basinstoke: Macmillan.

Mulligan, A. (2017) *Dog*. London: Pushkin Press.

Naidoo, B. (2000) *The Other Side of Truth*. London: Puffin.

Pennac, D., illustrated by B. Teckentrup, translated by S. Adams (2002) *Dog*. London: Walker.

Sanna, F. (2016) *The Journey*. London: Flying Eye.

Schwartz, J., illustrated by S. Smith (2017) *Town is by the Sea*. London: Walker.

Torday, P. (2013) *The Last Wild*. London: Quercus.

Torday, P. (2014) *The Dark Wild*. London: Quercus.

Torday, P. (2015) *The Wild Beyond*. London: Quercus.

INDEX